PETER HENSHAW

THE
BSA
BANTAM
BIBLE

ALL MODELS 1948-1971

Veloce

Other great books from Veloce –

www.veloce.co.uk

First published in June 2008 by Veloce Publishing Limited, 33 Trinity Street, Dorchester DT1 1TT, England. Fax 01305 268864/e-mail info@veloce.co.uk/web www.veloce.co.uk or www.velocebooks.com.
ISBN: 978-1-84584-159-1/UPC: 6-36847-04159-5

Contents

Introduction & acknowledgements

Introduction

The BSA Bantam is a phenomenon. In numerical terms, it's the most successful British bike ever built, and over 30 years after the last one left the production line, thousands are still on the road.

They say that your first motorcycle is like your first love – you never forget it. The Bantam was just that for a generation of British motorcyclists, and that's why the little bird is looked back on with such affection today. Of course, even the rose tinted memories also remember the intermittment electrics and feeble brakes, the jumping out of gear and time spent on roadside 'maintenance' that seemed to be part of Bantam ownership, especially when it involved an abused example, as many of them were.

Yet it was a tough little bird as well. Not only did Bantams carry a generation to and from work every day, but they proved capable of feats the original designer at DKW could never have envisaged. Bantams have crossed continents and climbed mountains. They have raced at the TT, around circuits, done scrambles and trials, even ridden the 'Wall of Death'.

The Bantam, as surely everyone knows by now, didn't start out as a British bike, but the British took it to their hearts, and for many who grew up in

The Bantam has been loved and cursed for generations. (Roger Fogg)

One of the last, a 1968 D14/4. (Roger Fogg)

the 1950s, '60s and '70s, it was part of adolescence. For them, the Bantam will always be associated with happy memories, and that's not a bad legacy to have.

Acknowledgements
This book could never have got off the ground without the help of a great many people. Roger Fogg took most of the pictures, kept a sharp lookout for Bantam stories, and generally kept me going; Nick Ward kindly allowed me to use his wonderful Bantam illustrations – these are works of art. Mike Jackson was helpful with sources and Peter Glover told me the story of how the Bushman came about. Michael Martin, who worked on developing the Bantam from 1965, was a mine of information.

Many prefer the simpler charms of an early D1. (Roger Fogg)

Spares man John Felan, better known to most as 'Bantam John' (01246 290021) was very generous with his time, spending most of an afternoon explaining the ins and outs of Bantam ownership. Annice Collett, of the VMCC Library, was likewise unstinting in her help. To Alan Brown of the Bantam Racing Club, thanks for your enthusiasm and help, also Colin Atkinson of the British Two-Stroke Owners Club and to George Sartin. Allan Ford introduced me to the world of Wall of Death Bantams and lent me some treasured pictures, while Peter Old provided many of the brochure illustrations. The staff at the British Postal Museum and Archive kindly allowed me to photograph GPO Bantams, and Mortons Media gave permission for road test quotes from *The Motorcycle* and *Motorcycling*. My brother David scanned some of the pictures – one of these days, I must buy a scanner myself.

Thanks also go to all those people who shared their Bantam memories: Hedley Sleep, Billy Simpkins, Joanie, John Bolam, Pete Kelly and Neil Sinclair. To those whose epic trips by Bantam are included: Peggy Iris Thomas, Arden Jensen, Brian Moore, Julian Preece, Maurice Smith and Ken Ascott. And also to those whose bikes were photographed for this book: Ian Thompson, Ray and Linda Freeman, Don Scott, Bette Barber, Ken Harvey, Morf, Tony Powell, Kevin Pethick, Terry Williams and Rick Howell amongst others.

There will be others, so apologies go to anyone who I wasn't able to track down – thank you, one and all.

Sadly, Alistair Cave, Works Manager of Small Heath in the Bantam years, died a few days before I could interview him. This book is dedicated to him, and to the women and men of BSA, who built the Bantam.

Why not visit Veloce on the web? – www.velocebooks.com
New book news • Special offers • Details of all books in print • Gift vouchers

6

Origins

Ancestors – cousins

Like most motorcycles, the BSA Bantam had identifiable ancestors, but only two of them were made by BSA! It also had a whole raft of cousins built around the world ... we'll come to those later.

If the Bantam had a spiritual ancestor from within the giant manufacturing plant of Small Heath, then there's one outstanding candidate: the 'Round Tank' got its memorable nickname from the shape of its cylindrical fuel tank. Launched in 1924, it cost less than £40, ready to ride. The Round Tank was also light, at 170lb, and simple (with just a two-speed gearbox and total-loss lubrication). A sidevalve 250cc single could push it up to a useful 45mph and give 120mpg. Buyers even had the choice of sports or touring handlebars.

The Round Tank was a huge hit, and 15,000 were sold in its first year.

By the end of its production run, BSA had added a three-speed box, pumped lubrication and drum brakes at both ends. When the Depression hit, Small Heath unveiled an 'economy' version of the Round Tank. You wouldn't have thought such a version was possible, but this one abandoned the oil pump for a cheaper gravity-fed system, and cut the price to an astonishing £33 15s. At 2007 prices, that's around £1400, or less than half the price of a modern 250cc scooter. So even by the standards of its time, the Round Tank was dirt cheap – not quite the proverbial 'cheaper than shoe leather,' but very nearly.

The Bantam's scavenged twin-loop two-stroke owed its existence to DKW. (Roger Fogg)

The Round Tank, of course, was a four-stroke, but BSA had a less happy experience with its first two-stroke – indeed, its only two-stroke before the Bantam. At the time, two-strokes didn't have a good reputation. They might have been simple and cheap to make, but they were also relatively crude, smoky, and without enough power to pull the skin off curdled milk, let alone something as substantial as a rice pudding. The mighty Villiers of Wolverhampton was the only two-stroke specialist, and sold its little engines to a whole host of smaller manufacturers.

BSA designed its own, and launched the result

at the 1927 Motorcycle Show at Olympia. Intended to undercut even the Round Tank, it had a specification that pre-empted the Bantam in some ways. The Model A had a 174cc unit construction engine, with petroil lubrication and magneto ignition. To keep the price as low as possible, it was festooned with cost-cutting measures: the cylinder head and barrel were one-piece cast-iron; the rigid frame had girder forks with no damping; there was no front brake, though the rear had two sets of shoes, operated independently so that BSA's first two-stroke complied with the letter of the law; the flywheel was exposed; and there was a hand change to select either of the gearbox's two speeds.

At £28 10s, the price was right, but the Model A's performance was pathetic and BSA thought better of it after making only a handful. It did try again the following year, relaunching the bike with an air cleaner, enclosed flywheel and the option of a three-speed gearbox, front brake and even electric lighting, but it still didn't attract buyers,

and BSA withdrew its two-stroke, giving up the whole thing as a bad job. Apart from an autocycle announced in 1939 and stymied by the war, it wouldn't think seriously about a two-stroke again for nearly 20 years.

In August 1944, with the outcome of World War II no longer in doubt, BSA's board of directors was considering its post-war strategy. The company had been kept busy on government engineering contracts right through the war, as well as supplying bikes like the venerable M20 sidevalve. The quickest route back to civilian production was to reintroduce the 1940 model range, and all of BSA's mainstream rivals were planning to do exactly the same thing.

That was all very well, but as Managing Director James Leek acknowledged, the 1940 line-up would begin to look outdated in the early post-war years. More to the point for the Bantam story, BSA had no small-capacity bike, but it would certainly need one for the post-war market. After six years of war, with much of its industry and

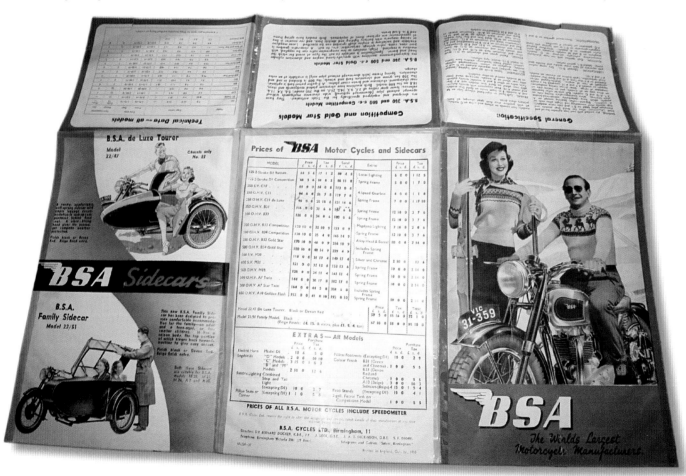

BSA may have been the "World's Largest" when the Bantam was launched, but not for much longer. (Roger Fogg)

transport infrastructure either bombed out or worn out, with petrol on ration and the need to 'export or die', austerity-era Britain would need cheap, basic transport, not Gold Stars.

Then things began to come together ... At that same August 1944 meeting where the need for a small bike was brought to the board's attention, it also considered tendering a contract for a Swedish company to supply small two-stroke engines. This, too, might have come to nothing had it not been for war reparations. The victorious Allies considered that Germany's impressive technological base was there to be shared out between them, and so designs for a whole variety were taken west (or east) after the end of the war, not that these were always welcomed; the VW Beetle was hawked around British car manufacturers, all of whom famously rejected it out of hand. With hindsight, their decision to decline what became the best selling car of all time looks daft, but, of course, this air-cooled, rear-engined device simply looked odd to British eyes.

The same fate nearly befell the Bantam. In this case, the hardware on offer was the DKW RT125, a ready-made two-stroke of up-to-date design. The drawings were shown to Villiers, which, for reasons of its own, decided not to take it up. Over at BSA, however, it was a different story: the company had little experience of designing two-strokes (and that wasn't good), but was facing the prospect of a lucrative engine contract, and a world that would very soon be demanding cheap, reliable transport. From the directors' point of view, to be presented with a ready-to-go little two-stroke machine on which the major design and development work had already been done was too good an opportunity to miss. So they said yes, and the Bantam was on its way.

The DKW connection

DKW (Dampf Kraft Wagen) had been founded back in 1919 by a Danish engineer named JS Rasmussen. And if BSA had been free to choose a two-stroke partner in more peaceful times, then it couldn't have done better than go with DKW. Put simply, the German company was a world leader in two-stroke technology.

DKW built its first bike in the early 1920s, and went on to specialise in a whole range of two-stroke racers. So determined was this effort that by 1939 DKW had the largest racing department in the world, with 150 staff dedicated to designing, building and developing race bikes. At the time, Auto Union and Mercedes were attempting to dominate motor racing for overtly political

The left-hand gearchange and kickstart identifies this as a DKW, not a Bantam. (Roger Fogg)

How it all began – the DKW RT125. (Gnu Free Documentation Licence)

CONTROLS

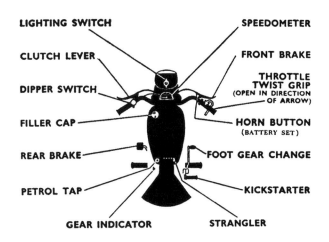

Bantams, like the DKW, were simple machines. (Roger Fogg)

The Bantam proved amenable to off-road adaptation.
(Roger Fogg)

reasons, and BMW was trying the same in four-stroke bike racing. DKW sought to make German engineering dominant in two-strokes.

By all accounts, it succeeded, and by the

1930s had built-up some impressive technical know-how. This was partly through patient refinement of the basic design of a piston-port two-stroke and partly through more radical developments such as supercharging and double piston designs. One DKW racing 250 made 49bhp, a staggering figure for the time.

Fortunately for DKW's mass production arm, this advanced thinking filtered down to the road bikes as well. DKW's factory at Zschopauer in Saxony was at one point the largest motorcycle plant in the world, and by 1939 the company had built over half-a-million machines. And one of the most successful was a little 125cc lightweight named the RT125 (RT for 'Reichstype').

It was simple but advanced, with a unit-construction engine and three-speed gearbox with flywheel magneto built in. Naturally, the little RT made use of DKW's two-stroke expertise, and designer Hermann Weber gave it Schnuerle type twin-loop transfer ports and a flat-top piston. This was superior to a traditional two-stroke, which used an odd 'deflector' on the piston top in an attempt to separate the incoming fresh charge and outgoing exhaust gases. This was a bugbear of early two-strokes – inevitably, some unburnt gases would escape straight through the exhaust port, while some exhaust fumes would linger inside the cylinder and dilute the fresh fuel/air mixture. The result was uneven running, low power and poor

Did DKW ever envisage that its design would be a favourite with English green-laners 70 years on? (Roger Fogg)

Many restoration projects start like this. (Roger Fogg)

efficiency. Dr Schnuerle's answer was to provide two transfer ports, one each side of the cylinder. As the fresh gases charged in from opposite sides, they would meet and swirl together, giving the exhaust gas a good chance to make its escape. Twin-loop scavenging, as it was known, didn't lead to perfect combustion, but was far more efficient than the old deflector system, with a lighter piston as icing on the cake.

With such advanced technology to back it up, the RT125 was a fine bike for its time, able to reach 56km/h – say, 35mph – and make a mere litre of fuel last 40km, which equates to well over 100mpg. Solid and robust, it also had considerable military potential, and 21,000 RTs were acquired by the Wehrmacht.

Fast forward a few years to a defeated Germany, and DKW's Zschopauer factory found itself in the Russian-occupied sector – what would become the Communist-controlled GDR. The DKW story then split in two. Zschopauer resumed motorcycle production, and would become MZ, while top-grade technicians such as Hermann Weber were shipped eastward to Russia. Weber was just a small part of a massive exodus of machine tools, know-how and brain power that was removed from Germany and taken east to benefit Russia. The Soviets of course, had experienced a brutal war at the hands of the Nazis, suffering millions of casualties – civilian as well as military – in resisting the Third Reich. To them, this was their own form of reparation.

Meanwhile, leaving Zschopau to the nascent MZ, DKW moved west to Ingolstadt in the American-occupied zone of Germany, and began making bikes again in 1949, with the RT125W ('W' for 'West') taking up where the original had left off. The RT and its descendants didn't last as long as the Bantam, but they were in production right through the 1950s. The 125 was replaced by an RT200 in 1951, capable of over 50mph, which added plunger rear suspension the following year. The 1953 RT175 had a new engine and four-speed gearbox, and a similarly updated 200 offered 11hp.

These 'Western' DKWs made an interesting comparison to the Bantam. They were undeniably better quality and very well equipped, with solid alloy control levers instead of pressed steel ones, a full chaincase, and an elegant cover over the Bing carburettor. The post-war DKWs were

more powerful than their BSA cousin to boot, and adopted a four-speed box over a decade earlier, despite which, the 1958 RT200 was actually cheaper than the equivalent 200cc James.

Ironically, none of this helped DKW survive. Germany's rapid post-war recovery saw motorcycle sales plummet as an increasingly affluent population opted for a new VW Beetle or NSU car instead of a bike. The Ingolstadt motorcycle business was merged with Victoria and Express in 1958, and the RT175 and 200 ceased production a couple of years later. So, whilst the Bantam might have been a DKW copy, it outlived the original by over a decade.

Now there's a sign of long life – tank badge almost worn away by generations of knees. (Roger Fogg)

Bantam cousins

BSA wasn't alone in copying the DKW. In fact, the RT125 must surely be the most copied motorcycle the world has ever seen, built in the USA, Poland, Germany (East and West), Japan and India. The closeness of the copying varied, and as the years went by, each was developed along its own path, though none ended up radically different to the original. It's said that the engine from any side of this extended family – whether BSA, Harley-Davidson, WSK ... whatever – would happily bolt straight into the frame of any other.

The Russian/ East German connection

With the old DKW factory at Zschopau (now in East Germany) nationalised and renamed as IFA, production resumed in 1946. The RT125 became the Mockba (or Maskva) M1A, at first with girder forks, and later with telescopics. It was also known as the MZ RT125. Production ceased in the 1950s, though arguably the MZs that followed in the same factory (and were in production right up to 1991) followed the same design philosophy. MuZ, as the revived company was known, also revived the RT125 name for its all-new four-stroke 125 in 2001.

The American connection

Of all the DKW cousins, that produced by Harley-Davidson seems the most unlikely. For over 40 years, the Milwaukee concern has produced nothing but the big V-twins with which its name is synonymous. Until 1978, it did sell a range of two-stroke trail bikes as well, but these were made in Italy, and were Harleys in name only. But the Model 125, or 'Hummer' as it later became, was a genuine Harley-Davidson, assembled in the same Milwaukee factory as the big twins. It was the smallest bike Harley ever built, and in all likelihood ever will.

Harley's reasons for taking on the DKW blueprints were exactly the same as those of BSA: it needed a small lightweight bike to serve the post-war market, and copying the RT offered a quick shortcut. And it certainly was quick, as Harley launched its Model 125 on 24th November 1947, at a dealer convention in Milwaukee, a full year before the Bantam went on sale.

Unlike the Bantam, the baby Harley retained girder forks, with rubber band suspension, though these were replaced by telescopics in 1951. It claimed 3bhp (significantly less than the first Bantam's 4.5bhp) and some traditionalist Harley dealers actually refused to sell this pipsqueak bike. Unlike the Bantam, it wasn't sold as a ride to work machine. Instead, the adverts were clearly aimed at clean living college kids and bobby-socked girls. Reflecting a more affluent market, it was expected to sell to teenagers who would quickly move on to a second-hand Ford or Chevy once they got their first job.

For 1953, Harley enlarged the two-stroke to 165cc, now with 5.5bhp and cleaner looking tinwork. Two years later, the 125 was reintroduced as the Hummer (named after Dean Hummer, the California H-D dealer who had sold most lightweights the previous year). These two soldiered on to 1960, when both were replaced by the Super 10, powered by an updated 165cc engine. That power unit was also used in Harley's one and only scooter, the Topper, which came with automatic transmission, but its square-rigged style looked clumsy next to a Vespa or Lambretta.

The range blossomed into three bikes in 1962, all of them with a 175cc development of the familiar two-stroke: the rigid-framed, stripped-down Ranger, road bike Pacer and trail bike Scat. But none of them were a match for the new generation of Japanese lightweights, and although Harley did introduce the restyled Bobcat in 1966, that was the end of the line for Harley's variation on the Bantam theme. It was dropped in favour of a new range of lightweights built by Aermacchi in Italy.

The Polish connection

The Bantam's Polish connection is complicated, because DKW-derived bikes were made at three different factories, though all of them were RT-inspired and shared many components. Production began in 1948 and was continued

Wico-Pacy generator cover on an early Bantam. (Roger Fogg)

This was Harley-Davidson's take on the DKW. (Michael Martin)

by the WFM, SHL and WKS factories, lingering on until 1985!

At first, this was just assembly of bought-in components, but by 1955 all parts except generators and carburettors were being made in-house. WFM built the engines, which it supplied to both WSK and SHL. But far from being a continuation of a pre-war design, the Polish 'DKWs' were well developed. WFM had experimental and racing departments, and was working on a prototype 250cc engine when it was unceremoniously ordered to stop making bikes and turn to optical instruments instead. Such were the

mysteries of the centrally planned Eastern Bloc. Telescopic forks and swingarm rear suspension featured from the mid-1950s, so the Polish bikes were being developed at about the same speed as the Bantam!

The bikes built by SHL were considered to be the best quality, and were also the most expensive, even offering a choice of colours with chrome panels. The later M06 development was the most popular of all, built by all three factories and powered by 125 and 148cc engines, the SHL version fitted with leading link Earles forks from 1959. The M06 was the bike that, with a final major

Special-use Bantams demanded special fittings – this is an ex-army machine. (Roger Fogg)

Token arty shot. The 'piled arms' tank badge was a reminder of BSA's own origins. (Roger Fogg)

update in 1971, soldiered on to 1985 with only cosmetic changes. Production totals are uncertain, but the Poles certainly built lots of Bantam cousins; an example is SHL's M11, a 175cc development made from 1962 to 1967, with production figures totalling 152,000 according to one source. It was licenced for production in India from 1963. WFM production is estimated at over 600,000 machines, and WSK 1.7 million, though not all of them were DKW derived.

The Indian connection
This was the Rajdoot Electronic, a licence-built version of the Polish SHL M11, built by Escort Yamaha Motors Ltd. The Indian bike was updated in later years, with 12-volt electrics and CDI ignition. The later 175cc Rajdoot Deluxe used the same bore and stroke dimensions as the 175cc Bantam.

The Japanese connection
Unlike the Bantam cousins in American and northern Europe, the one in Japan did not come about as a result of war reparations. Indeed, with Japan one of the defeated nations, it couldn't have been, and it isn't known how Yamaha acquired the DKW design. Still, the fact remains that Yamaha's first production bike was the YA-1, produced from 1954 and bearing a close resemblance to DKW's finest. Sold under the more poetic 'Red Dragonfly' name, the Yamaha was powered by a 123cc engine with the same bore

and stroke dimensions as the D1 Bantam, though it had a four-speed gearbox and a slightly larger 9-litre fuel tank.

The Redditch connection
There is one other member of the Bantam/DKW family that deserves a mention – the Royal Enfield Flying Flea. It was a case of the Third Reich's inhuman policies backfiring on them, and it happened like this ...

In 1938, the DKW motorcycle importer for Holland, Rotterdam-based RS Stokvis en Zonen, was happily selling the little RT100, a smaller version of the RT125, which was very popular there, but the Nazis discovered that the company had Jewish directors. They immediately confiscated the DKW franchise, handing it to Holland's DKW car importer; Stokvis en Zonen wasn't about to take this lying down – the board went straight to Redditch and asked if they could make something similar, if not identical, to the RT100.

Royal Enfield did just that, though not being familiar with the RT100's sophisticated Schnuerle twin-loop scavenging, it made a conventional two-stroke instead. That meant less power, and to produce the same as the RT100 it had to increase capacity to 125cc, so that's what it did. The frame was a straight copy of the RT, as was the rubber-band front suspension and even the silver-wing fuel tank side panels.

This was the Model RE, but only a few were built before October 1939 when war intervened,

DKWs were small, and so are Bantams. This is Ian Thompson and his D1. (Roger Fogg)

and the jigs and tooling were put into storage. They wouldn't stay there long. Arthur Bourne, editor of *The Motor Cycle*, had long been trying to persuade the British Army to make use of lightweight two-strokes, though it remained wedded to its 350cc four-strokes. Then, in early 1942, he was asked to give a demonstration, and brought along an RT100 as representative of the best German lightweight practice.

The effect on the top brass was instantaneous, as he later wrote: "On a Monday we took delivery of a machine, on the Tuesday we demonstrated in concert with WD types – to state that those who saw and rode the machine were amazed at its capabilities is putting it mildly. On the Wednesday, the machine was demonstrated to, and ridden by, a General, and on the Wednesday of the following week the production of such machines for military use was officially sanctioned."

Of course, the War Ministry could hardly place an order with DKW, but Royal Enfield was able to step in and offer to build its own Model RE. This became the Flying Flea, so-called because it was light enough to be parachute-dropped alongside troops, or carried to Arnhem or Normandy by glider. REs were also used as mechanical sheepdogs on the Normandy beaches, leading troops through cleared gaps in the defences. They

They're slim, too. (Roger Fogg)

were even carried on the back of tracked Bren carriers, as tenders.

Busy with other wartime commitments, Royal Enfield couldn't make as many Fleas as the Forces needed, so James helped out with its own version, the ML, powered by a 125cc Villiers engine. When peace returned, both the Enfield RE and James ML carried on as peacetime bikes. In fact, offered very soon after the end of the war, they pre-dated the Bantam by three years, and a descendent was built up to 1962. But compared to a Bantam D1, the RE gave away a whole horsepower, and was slow by comparison, which is saying a great deal! It also had a non-unit gearbox and hand gearchange, so as far as DKW copies went, the Bantam was truer to the original, and thus more advanced.

Why not visit Veloce on the web? – www.velocebooks.com
New book news • Special offers • Details of all books in print • Gift vouchers

15

2

D1: starting out

Development – launch – success

BSA had decided that DKW's RT was just the thing to meet its post-war needs, a well-proven bike of quality design, but that didn't mean it would rush straight into production. In fact, of all the Allied DKW copies, the Bantam was the last to go on sale. One rumour has it that the Parachute Regiment delivered a captured DKW to BSA as early as 1944, but according to Owen Wright, author of *BSA Bantam*, there's no evidence for this. What we do know is that an RT was delivered to BSA's Redditch experimental department in 1946, but it would be nearly two years before BSA's version finally went on sale, and then for export only.

Erling Poppe was the man in charge of the project at BSA, with Les Whittaker as chief draughtsman and assisted by an 18-year-old named John Garner, amongst others. Garner later recalled that the DKW in their workshop was a curious looking beast, in matt black with no badges, and hitched to a small box sidecar. Someone had already dismantled the engine, which had a dynamo and coil ignition, and the forks were pressed steel, with rubber band suspension.

The first job was to dismantle the whole bike and make new drawings, using Imperial measurements and Whitworth threads. These were used as the pattern for six complete engines, though even at this early stage, there were a few changes. The clutch drum was steel instead of the cast-iron used by DKW, there was an Amal carburettor, and room for a Lucas generator.

The new BSA engines were run up on the bench before being bolted into the original DKW frame and taken out into the open air for the first time. Almost immediately there were problems. The clutch centre seized on its shaft, which was rectified by specifying a bronze bush, and the crankshaft drive sprocket key sheared, the latter cured by a wider key. On the early prototypes, the outer drive side main bearing had no source of lubrication, though this was rectified for production, gearbox oil providing the lube. It was later improved still further with a dedicated oilway.

John Garner was tasked with giving the

BSA's take on the RT125 was right first time. (Roger Fogg)

prototype some serious road testing, and he rode it to the Bwlch-y-Groes pass in Wales. He made the climb three times, and thought that the piston had nipped up a few times. Back at the factory, they took the engine apart and found that the piston was scored and the second ring stuck in its groove. That could all be attended to, but what mattered more was that the little bike had kept going under duress. One of the Bantam's key strengths – its reliability – was already in place.

Testing continued through 1947, and one thing the team discovered was that the original Bing was significantly more efficient than the Amal intended for use. With the Bing bolted in, the prototype could manage 52mph flat-out, with the rider sitting up, and an impressive 140mpg at a steady 30mph.

How much simpler can a motorbike be? (Roger Fogg)

With the Amal in place, the equivalent figures were just 49mph and 128mpg. The obvious answer was to make a Bing copy, and a set of tools was ordered to do just that.

But then there were second thoughts, and it seems likely that cost considerations played a part. A Bing-copy carb would make the bike faster and more economical, but it would also cost money to tool up and get into production. The plan was dropped, and the prototype stuck to its Amal. In fact, as the whole project crept closer to an on-sale date, BSA's attention seems to have focused on cutting costs, and on the reaction of British riders to the little bike. So the planned Lucas

electrics were dropped in favour of the cheaper Wico-Pacy Geni-mag flywheel magneto, which generations of Bantam owners would see as a mixed blessing.

BSA also decided to reverse the primary drive layout, putting it on the right rather than the left. This had nothing to do with economics, and more to do with the fundamental conservatism of British motorcyclists. All British bikes had their gearlever and kickstart on the right, brake pedal on the left, but the prototype's were the other way round. This was thought to be too much for the average commuter, so the whole lot was swapped over. Of course, this also meant that the primary drive was

The D1's 123cc engine delivered a relatively relaxed 4.5bhp. (Roger Fogg)

1957 brochure cover, and the D1 Bantam hadn't changed yet (Weymouth Harbour still hasn't). (Peter Old)

now on the 'wrong' side (most British machines had it on the left) but at least the gear and kickstart sprouted from the correct side. The latter incidentally, was also unusual in that gears and kickstart were mounted concentrically, and both needed to be kept nice and tight if they weren't to strip the splines. CZ of Czechslovakia got round this conundrum by using just one reversible lever for both gear changing and starting.

The launch

March 1948 saw the first public acknowledgement that BSA was working on a two-stroke engine, though not a motorcycle to house it. A press release announced a new all-enclosed 123cc power unit, being supplied to contract. It was three months later that another press release finally made the new bike public, though at this point it was referred to as a plain 'D1' – the Bantam tag would come a few months later still. And despite all the efforts to give it a right-hand gearlever, the new bike was for export only. At the time, Britain

was bankrupt, heavily in debt to the USA, which had abruptly ceased the 'lend-lease' agreement when the war ended. Desperately short of foreign currency, it really was a case of 'export or die', and the D1 would play its part.

Perhaps it was the engine – Amal 261 carburettor apart – that had changed least, still a 123cc two-stroke with Schnuerle twin-loop

The bike announced in June 1948 exhibited all the development work that had gone on in the previous two years. Of all the DKW copies, it was probably the one with the most changes. As well as the reversed primary drive, there was a new all-welded frame, though still with a rigid rear end. The DKW's pressed steel forks and rubber band suspension had been dropped in favour of telescopics. Admittedly these were non-hydraulic forks, lubricated by grease rather than oil, and with no damping whatsoever, but teles nonetheless. Harley's 125 for example, didn't progress to telescopics for another three years.

Bette Barber, President of the Vintage Motorcycle Club, with her D1. (Roger Fogg)

Unlike other DKW copies, the BSA had telescopic forks. (Roger Fogg)

scavenging. Like the original, it had a distinctive 'pineapple' alloy head, with the sparkplug inclined backwards, the latter a Bantam recognition point that would last almost until the very end. The piston was a plain domed type, and both head and cast-iron barrel were clamped in place by four long bolts. This, too, was different from the usual British practice, which fastened the barrel via a flange and short studs.

Inside, the balanced full-circle flywheels and crankshaft were supported on three ball bearings – one on the generator side, two on the drive side – whose dimensions never changed in the Bantam's 23-year production run, during which time its power increased by 280 per cent! Oilways delivered lubricant to the inner two bearings, but the outer bearing on the drive side depended on gearbox oil for its lube. The big-end was a roller bearing.

On the left-hand side of the crank was the Wipac magneto generator, with its permanent magnet rotor keyed and bolted to the crankshaft itself. The stator plate around it held the lighting and ignition coils, with the contact breaker points mounted on the outside of the plate. The magneto meant no battery and direct lighting, and the

CLASS OF '48

Who was the typical motorcyclist in the year of the Bantam's introduction? A straw poll by Castrol revealed that 58 per cent of those interviewed were aged between 27-49, only a third were 17-25 and a mere 9 per cent were 50-60. Just over half stated they would grease their bike every 500 miles, a more slovenly 23 per cent every 1000 miles. Most were in favour of the latest telescopic forks, and better suspension was top of the list of improvements they'd like to see, followed by shaft drive and fuel consumption (thought equally desirable), closely followed by quietness, then weather protection. Only 4 per cent wanted more speed! (Or were more honest ...)

bike's audible means of alert was taken care of by a large bulb-horn mounted on the handlebars. To 21st century eyes, this looks like something from a vintage car (or bike), but, with no battery, how else was a BSA rider to let other road users know he/she was there?

On the right-hand side was the primary drive, a single-row non-adjustable chain, driving the six-spring, three-plate clutch, which in turn was controlled by a quick-thread helix pulled by the clutch cable. The three-speed gearbox, thanks to the primary drive being moved from left to right,

Heavily valanced mudguards were another feature of early Bantams. (Roger Fogg)

had a crossover shaft transferring drive to the left-hand sprocket. The gearlever return spring was located in the positive stop mechanism, in the bowels of the gearbox – which was why replacing it involved splitting the crankcases. A floppy, non-returning gearlever would thus strike terror, or at least gloom, into the hearts of a generation of Bantam owners. There was also a gear position indicator, mounted on the left at the front of the chainguard. Otherwise, the three-speed box was conventional, though unit construction was quite an advanced feature for 1948.

One of the immediate appeals of the D1 was that despite its size, it was quite clearly a sturdy little machine. There had been no skimping on

BSA 125 BANTAM MODEL D1

Dual seat and pillion footrests £4. 2s. 1d. extra.

Direct Lighting
£104. 18s. 11d.
including £17. 18s. 11d. purchase tax

Battery Lighting
£109. 15s. 5d.
including £18. 15s. 5d. purchase tax

Suspension. B.S.A. telescopic forks with flexible gaiters, plunger rear suspension on D1; hydraulically damped swinging-arm rear suspension with hydraulically damped telescopic front forks on D7.

Frame. Tubular cradle type; all welded on D1; of brazed and welded construction on D7. Spring-up central stand; B.S.A. dual seat and pillion footrests on D7. Lugs for steering head padlock on D7.

Finish. D1, Pastel green, alternatives Fuchsia red or Black; D7, Royal red, alternatives Sapphire blue or black; all frames and forks black. Cream panels and chrome strip on petrol tank; chrome panels with attractive plastic badges on D7 extra; hubs and brake cover plates black on D1, silver sheen on D7; chrome wheel rims; all other bright parts chromed.

General Dimensions. Wheelbase, D1, 50″, D7, 52″; ground clearance, D1, 4¼″, D7, 5¼″; overall length, D1, 77″, D7 81″; dry weight, D1, 180 lb., D7, 224 lb.

Extra Fittings (Prices include P.T.) Legshields £2. 1s. 1d; Prop stand £1. 0s. 6d; Safety bars, D1, £1. 13s. 2d; D7, £3. 12s. 5d. On D1, B.S.A. dual seat and pillion footrests, £4. 2s. 1d. Whitewall tyres D1, £1. 6s. 6d., D7, £1. 9s. 6d. On D7, Chrome tank panels £3. 10s.

Charming old world cottages at Welford-on-Avon.

No machine in the history of motor-cycling has achieved such world-wide popularity as the Bantam, a thoroughly reliable lightweight of proven performance. So easy to ride, it is the ideal motor cycle for the beginner and the obvious choice for daily transport. In price, economy, ease of handling and maintenance the Bantam has no equal.

Later model D1, in optional Fuschia Red and with plunger rear end (by now standard). (Peter Old)

First and last – D1 contrasts with red and chrome B175.
(Roger Fogg)

the wheel size, a full 19in, it had a decent 50in wheelbase and the all-welded tubular frame was motorcycle-style rather than pressed steel. In short, it looked like a real motorbike in miniature, which tended to instill confidence, and it certainly had more stable handling than a small-wheeled scooter. The new BSA looked clean and neat, with its fully valanced mudguards, tidy handlebar layout and unit engine/gearbox. The half-width brakes were again motorcycle-style, as was the solo sprung saddle and luggage rack.

And finally, despite austerity, despite most motorcycle makers' attachment to any colour you liked so long as it was the same as Henry Ford's Model T, the D1 came in a very fetching pastel green – the famous Mist Green – which contrasted with a cream panel on the tank. There was no chrome, but the little BSA arguably didn't need it. Considering its origins – a copy of a pre-war design – the new bike had a class all of its own. Despite looking like a serious motorbike, it also had a loveable appeal, something it shared with the Morris Minor announced the same year, that would endear it to thousands of riders.

So it all looked good, and BSA had evidently taken its time developing that partly-dismantled DKW into a production bike. What it didn't do was draw attention to the DKW connection. According to author Barry Ryerson (whose book *The Giants of Small Heath* is probably the best analysis of the long-term reasons why BSA eventually went under) there was no reference to the Bantam's DKW ancestry in any official literature. In fact, he maintains that the story was only broken by the BSA Owners Club magazine, *The Star*, years later. Of course, a basis in German engineering would be trumpeted from the rooftops now, but only three short years after the end of the war, things

Rigid rear end was common on commuter bikes in 1948.
(Roger Fogg)

were very different. There was arguably more pride in 'Britishness' then as well, and the assumption was that British had to be best. British, German or hybrid, whatever the Bantam was, what did the British public and press think of it?

The show
BSA didn't have long to wait to find out, as the D1's 'export only' status lasted a mere five months, until it was unveiled at the Earls Court Show in

November. It was quite an event. Attendance at that show broke all records, with 130,000 visitors flocking to see the wares of 29 British manufacturers. All of them would have gazed with longing at the Vincent-HRD V-twin, the fastest production bike in the world, or at the Triumph Speed Twin or maybe BSA's own Star Twin, a high-compression sports version of the A7 500cc twin, but few could afford any of those. Instead, they were more likely to budget for one of the many Villiers-powered commuters, or Royal Enfield's RE, which had covered itself in wartime glory as the Flying Flea, or perhaps the neat-looking little two-stroke that was proudly displayed on the BSA stand, and which now had a name slightly more evocative than the simple 'D1' – the Bantam.

Guest of honour at the show was none other than 'Monty', less well known as Lord Montgomery, or, if you insist, Field Marshal the Viscount Montgomery of Alamein KG, GCB, DSO. "The cycle and motorcycle industry of the United Kingdom may be held up as an example of what British workmanship can and should achieve," he declared, adding that Britain made more bikes

than any other country in the world. "I would add that you can claim without fear of contradiction to be one of the few United Kingdom industries which is recognised to be supreme in its particular sphere." Monty visited the BSA stand, though there's no record of what he thought of the Bantam. He was presented with a new Sunbeam S7 – it had been his birthday the day before, and in his speech revealed that his first bike had been a Sunbeam in 1911.

How did the Bantam compare to other bikes at the show? It's easy to forget that its basic design was already ten years old by this time – had six years of war, plus BSA's development time, seen it fall behind? Of 122 powered two-wheelers at that show, the cheapest (excepting mopeds) was the Aberdale autocycle at £39 14s, and most expensive was the Vincent, at £400. There were only four bikes over 600cc, but below that engine sizes were fairly evenly spread, with 500cc the most common. There were plenty of two-strokes (44 bikes out of the total) and all but 30 were singles. The vast majority used magneto electrics, with just ten offering the advance of a coil, while only

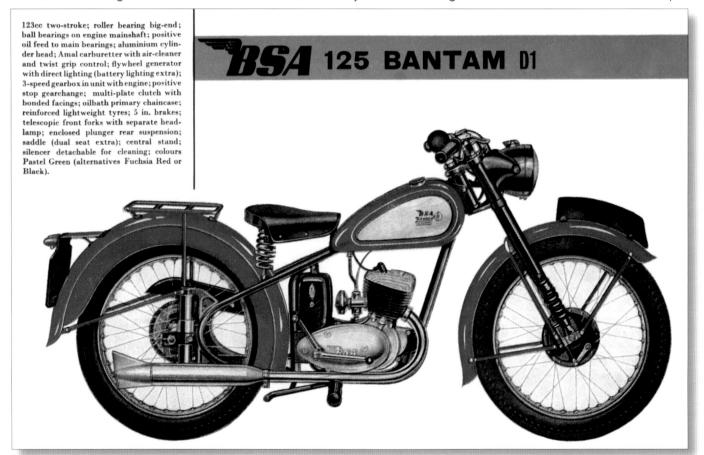

123cc two-stroke; roller bearing big-end; ball bearings on engine mainshaft; positive oil feed to main bearings; aluminium cylinder head; Amal carburetter with air-cleaner and twist grip control; flywheel generator with direct lighting (battery lighting extra); 3-speed gearbox in unit with engine; positive stop gearchange; multi-plate clutch with bonded facings; oilbath primary chaincase; reinforced lightweight tyres; 5 in. brakes; telescopic front forks with separate headlamp; enclosed plunger rear suspension; saddle (dual seat extra); central stand; silencer detachable for cleaning; colours Pastel Green (alternatives Fuchsia Red or Black).

BSA 125 BANTAM D1

The Plunger D1 remained in production right up to 1963. (Peter Old)

seven had shaft drive. A minority clung to a hand gearchange and nearly half had unit-construction, while 83 bikes out of the total had rigid rear ends.

All of which made the Bantam (two-stroke, unit construction, footchange, rigid rear) a fairly typical machine. With undamped forks, magneto electrics and that rigid rear end, it might seem crude from a 21st century perspective, but the Bantam was a modern design by Britain's 1948 standards, though by no means radical.

It was also cheap (see box). The little BSA's basic price was just £60, but purchase tax had to be added to that, plus 17s 6d road tax. And although BSA listed the Smiths speedometer as an extra at £3 3s 6d, it was in fact compulsory, so you had to have one of those. At £76 4s 0d ready to ride away (let's assume your friendly dealer has included a tank of petroil to seal the deal), the Bantam was significantly cheaper than 125cc rivals like the Francis Barnett Merlin (£85 1s 10d) or the Tandon (£90 3s 2d). Convert that into 2007 prices, and the first Bantam cost the equivalent of just over £1800, which would make it about the same as the very cheapest Italian 125cc scooters now on the market. So even at Earls Court, the BSA was good value.

Back in 1948, only the infamous Flying Flea managed to undercut the Bantam, and then by less than £3. At the other end of the scale was the Velocette LE, at a whopping £126 7s 4d; of course, this was a far more sophisticated machine, with its shaft drive and quiet, well-mannered, water-cooled four-stroke flat-twin. If you could afford one of those, it's unlikely you'd be giving the Bantam and its cheap and cheerful chums much of a second glance anyway ...

So how did the early Bantam compare to the only new 125 that managed to sell for a lower price? Fifty years later, Peter Watson sought to find out for *Classic Bike*, comparing a restored D1 to a Royal Enfield RE, and came to a very definite conclusion. He wrote that the RE felt "like a pre-war autocycle with an oversize engine", whereas the Bantam was "a small motorcycle rather than a 125cc moped."

The reasons weren't hard to find. Where the Bantam had telescopic forks, the RE clung to girders with rubber band suspension, straight copies of the pre-war DKW it was based on. The Enfield also clung onto an outmoded hand gearchange, much slower and less easy to use than the Bantam's foot change. It gave away a whole horsepower to the Bantam as well (which when dealing with sub-5bhp figures, is a fair old whack), and its lowly power rating was further hampered by the big gap between second

1948 PRICES (INCLUDING PURCHASE TAX)
Royal Enfield RE 'Flying Flea' £73 13s 3d
BSA Bantam D1 £76 4s 0d
James 122cc standard £83 11s 0d
Francis Barnett Merlin £85 1s 10d
Excelsior Universal £85 14s 6d
Tandon £90 3s 2d
Velocette LE £126 7s 4d

and top on the three-speed gearbox. Peter Watson found that the D1 would forge ahead by comparison, that extra horsepower making all the difference. The RE's 4in front brake was described as "absolutely pathetic", and the conclusion was inescapable – for an extra £3 over the price of an RE, the 1948 Bantam was a bargain.

The press

Britain had just two bike magazines in those days – *The Motor Cycle* and *Motorcycling*, otherwise known as the "blue 'un" and the "green 'un" respectively. Both were given a Bantam to test shortly before the Earls Court Show – BSA could hardly do otherwise, because to favour one magazine would have poisoned relations with the other one. The magazines, in their turn, did their best not to rock the boat with road tests where criticism wasn't just veiled, but hidden behind the linguistic equivalent of reinforced concrete.

Very nice replica of a trials Bantam, an ex-GPO bike bought by Roger Fogg and built by Brian Slark of the Barber Museum in the USA. It was presented to Irene Smith (wife of Jeff) on her retirement from the AHRMA: Irene rode trials on a Bantam as a young woman. (Roger Fogg)

"Attractive Lightweight Now Available on Home Market: Exceptional Economy", headlined *The Motor Cycle*'s test. It praised the performance ("a very high standard"), the lack of oil leaks ("most satisfactorily clean") and the clutch (which took up drive "smoothly and sweetly"). The testers found that the Bantam could reach 47mph flat-out and keep up an indicated 40-45mph on the open road. Like just about every Bantam road tester since, they were impressed by the economy, measuring 128mpg at a steady 40mph, 160mpg at 30mph and a spectacular 192mpg at 20mph. In 1948, as it always would be, fuel economy was one of the Bantam's strongest points.

The reviewers did note "a slight roughness in the transmission at speeds between 14 and 22mph in top gear" and that upward gearchanges between the widely spaced ratios couldn't be rushed. What wasn't mentioned (though thousands of Bantam riders would discover) was the big gap between second gear and top in the three-speed box. But *The Motor Cycle* couldn't find a polite way of describing the Bantam's exhaust note. It was, it said, plain and simple "noisy".

Motorcycling didn't test the same Bantam D1 (the registration was JOF 312 instead of *The Motor Cycle*'s JOF 311) and clearly didn't performance test it either, with no acceleration or steady-speed mpg figures. It quoted an indicated top speed of 54mph, suggesting that the D-shaped Smiths speedo was over-reading a little. However, it obviously had some fun, finding that the Bantam's

tractability and decent ground clearance made it happy to tackle 'cross-country', or what we would call green-laning. "The BSA's light weight, generous ground clearance and handleability proved it to be a mount eminently suitable for the man who tackles such conditions from necessity and not from choice." It also loved the brakes (which were tested, recording a 22ft stop from 30mph) and the forks ("most comfortable"). Oddly, compared to *The Motor Cycle*'s description of the Bantam's vocal exhaust, it described the note as "most subdued." Which was right?

Either way, and even given the gentlemanly standards of the time, the journalists were genuinely impressed by the new Bantam. Here was an up-to-date lightweight that rode well, sipped fuel at a miserly 120mpg or so, and was cheaper than all but one of its rivals. It was a good start.

The public

Over the next few years, the public as well as the press became familiar with the Bantam. They took an instant liking to the little two-stroke which was so easy to ride, yet fast enough to keep up with traffic of the time, and was, of course, dirt cheap to run. Better still, it kept on running. Until 1954, the bottom end relied entirely on petroil for its lube, but by the standards of contemporary two-strokes, was remarkably tough and long-lived. Word soon got round, with every Bantam selling as soon as it hit the showroom floor.

One of the bike's strengths was that it appealed to just about everyone. It was too cheerful to be seen as a middle-aged man's bike by the young; too sensible to be dismissed as a flash and short-lived speedster by the ride-to-work chaps. All ages, both sexes, private buyers and fleets such as the GPO, gas boards and even the Forestry Commission found the Bantam ideal. Best of all, it was fun. You didn't have to be skilled, or experienced, and certainly not rich, to enjoy a Bantam, and thousands of people did just that.

By May 1951, just two-and-a-bit years after that first Earls Court appearance, BSA had sold 50,000 D1s; after four years, the Bantam total hit six figures. It was a world record for motorcycle production (Honda was only just getting off the ground in 1953) and testament to the Bantam's innate qualities.

There were, of course, teething troubles, one of which was down to the that wide-ratio gearbox. Bantams were often used for short trips, and the bike's tractability encouraged gentle riders to trickle along at low revs in the relatively high top gear. So, on short rides to work, the engine never warmed up, allowing condensation to build up in

The D1 Competition soon joined the roadster. (Roger Fogg)

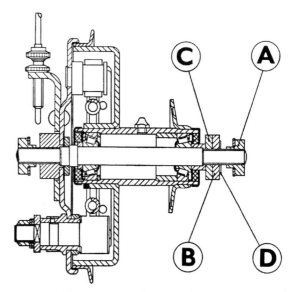

The Competition D1 came with an adjustable roller-bearing front hub. (Billy Simpkins)

'Younger brother of the B32 and B34 BSA Competition models.' (Peter Old)

the crankcase and eventually rust on the main bearings.

One Wilf Baxter of Castle Gresley near Burton-on-Trent had just this problem, with just one mile to ride to work each day. His D1 suffered premature main bearing failure more than once. Wilf had no formal qualifications, but he was a natural engineer, and realised what the cause was. His solution was to drill and tap a hole into each side of the crankcase, and fit a grease nipple. Each morning, before riding to work, he would give each nipple a squirt of oil, and never had any further trouble. An extreme solution, but it worked.

The Bantam appealed just as strongly to men of the cloth as to amateur engineers, and this one (an anonymous 'Motorcycling Minister') wrote to *The Motor Cycle* about his experiences: "I am the minister of a working-class congregation, and my little BSA Bantam has drawn me closer to my flock where a car might have set me apart ... In my sort of congregation, there are inevitably experts who will give help whenever it is needed. As for the Youth Club, the little machine, as a topic of conversation, has already broken the ice – with the girls no less than

the boys ... The Bantam does all I want it to do, for I have no desire for speed ... I have used the Bantam for conferences 250 miles away ... The amount that the engine will withstand makes me marvel."

Nevertheless, the motorcycling minister did have a few problems with his Bantam, but, as he found on a tour of the Western Isles, even this had a side benefit: "I had the misfortune to be on the loneliest part of Mull when a mudguard stay broke, fouled the chain and snapped it. Having no spare link, I pushed the machine for 15 miles (but) had I reached my destination, Iona, without a hitch, I would not know a soul on Mull, but now I remember the overwhelming kindness of some of the inhabitants."

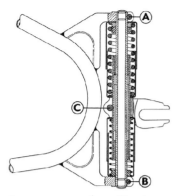

Plunger suspension offered limited movement. (Billy Simpkins)

First changes
Motorcycling's first road test of the Bantam had discovered what a useful off-road bike it was, which hinted at its future sideline as a farmer's runaround, especially in Australia. But if BSA had known nothing of the D1's off-road potential, it lost no time in making the most of it. The D1 Competition was launched at the 1949 Earls Court Show, and though mechanically very similar to the road bike, it did have some useful changes to make it more usable on the rough stuff. Most noticeable was the modestly upswept exhaust to increase ground clearance. There was a decompressor screwed into the cylinder head, a folding kickstart (the standard bike's non-folding lever was a nuisance on the road, doubly so when standing up through tricky going). Unvalanced mudguards saved a bit of weight, and a 58-tooth rear sprocket lowered the overall gearing. Not many Competitions were made, which makes them sought-after today, but

Rigid rear end, left-hand filler cap, unfinned silencer = early D1. (Roger Fogg)

they pointed towards the Bantam's bright future in off-road sport.

At the same time, plunger rear suspension was offered as an option. It was a sort of halfway house between a rigid rear and a swingarm, with opposed springs and sliding yokes carried in the hub, allowing about three inches of movement. Just like other plunger rear ends, that of the Bantam was simple and relatively crude, but did give a modicum of comfort when compared to no springing at all. It worked quite well at moderate speeds and if kept well-greased, but the plunger was really only a stopgap before the rapidly approaching swingarm became standard. There was a half-hearted attempt to name the plunger Bantam the D2, and some sprung frames were produced numbered YD2 instead of the rigid YD1. They soon reverted to YD1, but with the letter 'S' added.

Alongside the plunger option, BSA offered a Bantam De-Luxe, which had the plunger frame plus Lucas battery electrics in place of the Wipac magneto. This might have been an attempt to offer the Bantam buyer more sophisticated electrics, but according to Owen Wright, the truth had more to do with Wico-Pacy's inability to keep up with the demand for flywheel magnetos from BSA. To give Wipac a chance to catch up, BSA ordered 5000 sets from Lucas. As well as a generator, this brought coil ignition, and having a six-volt battery meant lights running independent of engine revs, plus an electric horn and brakelight. It was also the only Bantam sold with an ignition key.

The De-Luxe Bantam cost £6 more than the rigid Wipac-equipped one, and though not

Legshields were de rigueur for early 1950s commuters, and surprisingly effective. (Roger Fogg)

everyone liked the extra complication, the Lucas setup was a genuine improvement. It only lasted until 1953, and in the meantime an improved Wipac Series 55 Mk8 generator replaced the original Geni-mag. This came in both direct lighting and battery form, and was another step forward. A giveaway recognition factor is the cast-in BSA logo on the external cover plate.

Motorcycling tested a Bantam De-Luxe in Febrary 1950. It thought that it had appeared in response to requests from owners set on long-distance touring, who would appreciate the greater comfort of the plunger rear end, and better lights on long trips. The idea of long distance Bantam riding wasn't, and isn't, as fanciful as it sounds, and only a year or so after its launch, owners were already taking their Bantams on high-mileage adventures (see chapter 10).

The magazine was predictably impressed with the De-Luxe's special features. The plunger gave "a comfortable ride, entirely free from the pitching that is, at times, apparently inseparable from short-wheelbase, lightweight mounts." It even liked the handling, though not everyone would enjoy the variable geometry that plunger suspension could bestow. As for the battery lights, they were bright enough "to make night riding almost as comfortable as daytime cruising". An electric horn was

part of the deal, perhaps more effective but certainly less fun than the bulb-horn. "BSA Cycle Co Ltd, Small Heath, Birmingham," concluded this test of the De-Luxe, "may well feel proud of the manner in which the 'Bantam' has won its spurs."

Motorcycling also managed a miserly 179mpg at a steady 30mph, and with petrol still on ration this played a big part in the Bantam's early success. In 1950, a group of Australians had organised an ACU-observed test to see just how little fuel the BSA could use. It was all done properly. The importers delivered twelve cases to the Australian ACU, all unopened since being nailed down at Small Heath, and each containing three Bantams. The officials selected one case, and the three bikes inside were assembled under their supervision. Each Bantam was then run in for 200 miles, then set off on a 19 mile open road circuit to test either mph or mpg. One Bantam covered 510 miles in 12 hours, averaging 42.5mph and managed 48.5mph on one of the 19 mile laps. Another, ridden with economy in mind, and averaging less than half that speed, made 213.3mpg, and that was using standard jetting in the Amal.

Figures like these became less relevant as petrol came off ration and an increasingly affluent society began to demand more flash, pizazz and performance. Yet the basic 123cc Bantam clung on right up to 1963. By then its main customer was the Post Office, which in the bike's final year bought 600 of the 709 D1s produced. But the D1 Bantam had done its job: perfect for austerity Britain, it not only provided cheap, easy-to-use transport, but it was fun to ride. The Bantam was on its way.

3

D3: good morning, Major

An all-new two stroke – a bigger Bantam – the GPO story
If Hermann Meier had had his way, then the Bantam would have been replaced, or at least supplanted, by an all-new range of lightweight two-strokes in the mid-1950s. Despite building Britain's best-selling two-stroke, BSA knew very little about valveless engines. Before the Bantam, it hadn't built a two-stroke motorcycle for 20 years, and even the little rooster hadn't added much to Small Heath's know-how. The company had made plenty of changes in transforming the pre-war DKW RT125 into the post-war Bantam, but nothing that really delved into how this particular two-stroke worked. With its twin-loop scavenging, it was reasonably clean-running and very fuel-efficient, and, for 1948, that was enough.

However, someone at BSA evidently recognised the need for more in-depth, two-stroke expertise. Hermann Meier, the German tuner who would be instrumental in preparing the very quick Ariel Arrow ridden to seventh place in the 1960 250cc Lightweight TT, certainly fitted the bill. According to Michael Martin, a long-time BSA development engineer, Meier got the job partly because he could naturally read German and all the serious two-stroke research papers were in that language. Better still, he was backed by some very big guns at BSA, including Bert Hopwood, then chief engineer at Small Heath. Meier's job was to develop a new range of two-strokes that owed nothing to the Bantam. He asked for the help of

Compare and contrast: Pastel Grey D3 next to a Mist Green D1. (Ken Ascott)

Plunger D1, or 148cc D3? Grey paintwork, and Bantam Major tank badge, makes it the latter. (Roger Fogg)

Doug Hele, the fine development engineer who did so much to improve the post-war Triumph/BSA twins and triples, but that turned out to be a little ambitious. Instead, the young Bernard Hooper was assigned to him. Hooper had joined BSA at Redditch in 1952, was a gifted designer, and, more to the point for Meier, his heart was in two-strokes. "I wanted to work with Hermann," Hooper later recalled (interviewed in *Classic Bike*, January 1991), "because he really knew about two-strokes."

He drew up a complete range of all-new machines. They would have pressed steel frames, with a four-speed unit-construction two-stroke of 125, 150 or 175cc. The single-cylinder would be mounted almost flat, 15 degrees from the horizontal, like contemporary Moto Guzzis, and Bernard Hooper was full of enthusiasm for the concept: "I thought, this is going to be fantastic. They were really quite sporty bikes."

But it never happened. Even as prototype engine castings began to arrive, the whole project was unceremoniously cancelled. BSA had financial problems at the time, and a boardroom revolt led to the ousting of chairman Sir Bernard Docker, while long-time MD James Leek retired. At the same time, BSA was trying to push its Beeza scooter into production, and amidst the general tumult, it's not surprising that ambitious plans for a complete new range of bikes were dropped. As for the Beeza, that never did make it to the showrooms. Hooper and Meier were unimpressed by its 198cc four-stroke engine in any case, and fitted a 148cc Bantam unit which proved to be more powerful and "better all round", according to Hooper, "but the management wouldn't accept it."

As a two-stroke enthusiast, the young Bernard Hooper was well aware that in Germany and Italy two-stroke technology was forging ahead, whereas the Bantam, based on a pre-war design, had no significant developments at all. There were some tentative plans. When Hooper joined BSA in 1952, he took over an existing project to apply automatic oiling to the Bantam, but thought that the system being tested was inferior to that on his pre-war Velocette GTP. Autolube projects for the Bantam would come and go throughout its life, but none of them reached production. Hooper also designed a four-speed gearbox for the Bantam, something else that would have greatly extended its appeal and helped it keep up with the Continental competition. And that was something that BSA needed to do. Long before it became dependent on the USA market for big bikes, BSA was an export-driven company. In 1948, three-quarters of its production went abroad, and six years later, well after the 'export or die' period,

The Bantam Major carried on with the simple Wipac electrics. (Roger Fogg)

Small brakes now had slightly more performance to cope with. (Roger Fogg)

it was still sending everything from Bantams to Golden Flashes to over 150 countries, from Alaska to Samoa. But from the management's point of view, the Bantam was still selling well as a simple machine with a very low price, so the four-speed and auto oiling Bantams were shelved. However, one of Bernard Hooper's projects did reach fruition – the 148cc Bantam.

The Major

The 123cc D1 Bantam had done extraordinarily well, but while 4.5bhp and a top speed of 47mph might have been enough for austerity Britain, they were looking increasingly inadequate. Buyers were more affluent now, the country starting a long haul towards the 'never had it so good' years of the

'Shortens every distance but the one between refills.' (Peter Old)

main bearings was improved by adding a supply from the primary drive. To stiffen up the whole assembly, two extra crankcase fixing screws were added.

This all amounted to 5.2bhp at 5000rpm, a 16 per cent increase which was enough to nudge the top speed over 50mph, given the legendary 'favourable conditions'. As well as the extra oomph, the Bantam Major offered more substantial forks, borrowed from the 250cc C10, now with sythentic rubber inserts to provide some

late '50s. The typical Bantam buyer was more likely to take his/her bike touring as well. They wanted more power, and it arrived in October 1953 as the 148cc D3 Bantam Major.

It might only be a modest increase, but staying below 150cc kept the Bantam in the cheap road tax bracket. Increasing the bore to 57mm delivered the extra capacity, leaving the engine still slightly undersquare, but that wasn't the only change. To cope with the extra power, the cylinder barrel was made thicker, with more generous finning; the transfer ports were enlarged and the flywheels were beefed-up (actually the same type as used on Bantams with Lucas electrics), as was the big-end. There was a larger $^{11}/_{16}$in bore Amal carburettor, and lubrication of the

Climb every mountain – as long as you ride a BSA. (Peter Old)

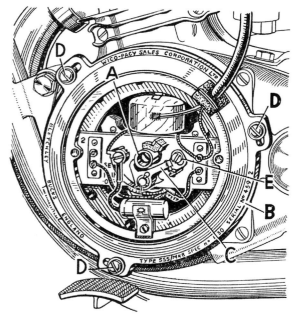

Wico-Pacy contact breaker points needed looking after.
(Billy Simpkins)

Did any tennis-playing bright young things ride Bantams?
(Peter Old)

damping. There was also a headlamp cowl, and a new silencer featured a detachable finned tail, enabling one to remove the baffles at decoke time. This made that job a whole lot easier, if no less messy than usual. The front mudguard had less valancing than before, while the fuel filler cap moved from the left-hand to the right-hand side of the tank. The latter was a sensible move, to prevent owners pouring neat oil into the tank, straight through the left-hand fuel tap and into the carburettor, where it would clog up the passages.

The D3 came with the plunger frame only, and there was a Competition variant as well, but the original D1 carried on alongside it, with many of the same changes. There was an attempt to relabel it the 'Bantam Minor', though this never caught on. Proud owners of new Bantam Majors needn't have worried though: no Bantam expert could mistake their bike, in Pastel Grey and with appropriate badging, for a humble Mist Green D1. It would soon, along with the D1, acquire a splash of chrome as well, on trim strips hiding the fuel tank seam, and on the wheel rims.

The Major evidently wasn't as eagerly awaited as the D1, as *The Motor Cycle* didn't publish a test until five months after the launch, and *Motorcycling* over a year after that. If there was one thing they agreed on (though of course, neither was so impolite as to draw attention to the fact), it was that the Major was only slightly faster than the D1. *The Motor Cycle* managed a top speed of 51mph (with a one-way best of 53mph)

just 4mph more than the original Bantam, and 0-30mph acceleration was cut from 6.8 seconds to 6.6. Despite the extra capacity, the 148cc had a narrower power band than before, and since the more substantial forks and engine internals added weight, the power-to-weight ratio was actually down on the D1. The gearing was unchanged, but the 44lb weight increase had its own effect. Even the wind could knock the big-engined Bantam back noticeably. *Motorcycling*'s test began with a run from Silverstone to Cambridge, and the rider was delighted to find that the D3 held an indicated 47-51mph all the way ("where road and gradient permitted"). Next morning though, battling into the strong breeze, cruising speed was down to less than 42mph, with a change down to second needed if the bike was baulked to 35-40mph.

Nevertheless, there was a small but useful increase in urge, and *The Motor Cycle* found that the D3 would keep up an indicated 45mph on an undulating main road, and in 1954 that 0-30mph time was still fast enough to make the Bantam quicker than the average car. It liked the cold starting (first or second kick), the "short and positive" gear change, and thought the steering and road-holding was "above criticism". For the first time, it observed that handling was limited by scraping footrests, a complaint that would be echoed by Bantam riders and road testers for years to come.

Reading between the lines, the riding position was thought too cramped for taller riders, and the horn note "could, with advantage, have been more penetrating". It loved the brakes though: "ample stopping power ... light and smooth in operation." Being heavier and more powerful than the D1, the Major naturally drank more as well – *Motorcycling* reckoned on just over 90mpg for that dash to Cambridge – but the big Bantam was still a pretty frugal machine.

"Attractive two-stroke lightweight with excellent steering, roadholding and braking," headlined *The Motorcycle*, concluding that the bigger engine broadened the bike's appeal: "price and fuel consumption are higher than those for the smaller Bantam, but these factors are offset by the one-fifty's enhanced acceleration and speed performance, and its great suitability for carrying a pillion passenger."

A choice of colour
There were few changes for 1955, though one in particular would spoil the Bantam's reputation for interchangeability. The cylinder barrel spigot was enlarged, with a spacing collar added between the left-hand flywheel and adjacent main bearing. That meant a new crankcase casting as well as a new barrel, so pre- and post-1955 barrels and cases were not interchangeable. It was, and is, a rare chink in the Bantam's 'everything fits everything' adaptability.

Most Bantam buyers that year however, would have taken more notice of the new range

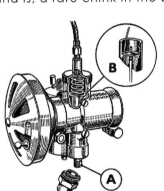

The tiny Amal carburettor wasn't as frugal as the DKW's Bing, but still delivered over 100mpg. (Billy Simpkins)

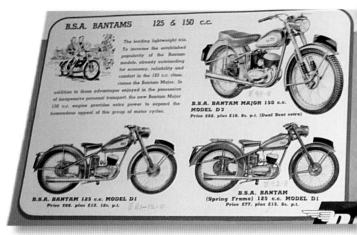

The Bantam range, circa 1956. (Peter Old)

of colours. For the first time, one could have a Bantam not just in any colour you wanted, so long as it was Mist Green. The new choices were black or maroon, both with the same cream tank panel that Bantams had always worn. As standard, the D1 continued with its traditional Mist Green (and in fact most D1 buyers stuck with this classic D1 colour) and the D3 its Pastel Grey. None of the colour choices were exactly flamboyant, but what with these and the new chrome wheel rims and tank trim, the Bantam was finally taking a tentative step into the more colourful 1950s.

There were bigger changes the following year, when the D1 and D3 Competition bikes were phased out, as was the rigid-frame D1 and plunger D3. As standard, the Bantam Major now had a swingarm rear end, with twin Girling shock absorbers mounted on a swingarm which used rubber bushes. The altered rear frame enabled the fitment of bigger triangular side panels with a toolkit and/or battery. The latter was still an option, many Bantams leaving the factory with

FANCY FOUR WHEELS?
If you were looking to move on to four wheels in 1956, and couldn't be tempted even by a Bantam Major, then one of the cheapest new options was a two-seater Bond Minicar at £278 13s 2d. You could buy two Bantams for the same money, and have enough change left over for a fortnight in Bournemouth. On the other hand, the Bond was a halfway house to car-style weather protection, and still claimed 85mpg. For marrieds with children, there was a four-seat Family model at just over £300. And both could be driven on a motorcycle licence.

'Motorcycle Value at its Best' – the Bantam was part of a whole range of BSA singles. (Peter Old)

simple direct lighting. Along with the new rear end was a quite graceful tapered silencer, which had the same detachable finned rear section but was said to improve engine breathing. Finally, a dual seat and pillion footrests were standard – the dual seat had previously been optional.

The swingarm set up certainly improved comfort and handling, and when *The Motor Cycle* tested a swingarm Major in July 1956, it thought the "steering first class and cornering effortless", though once again the grinding footrests were condemned! It noted that the Girling shocks weren't adjustable, and were just about right for two "normal-sized" adults, but firm when riding solo. Of course, the swingarm also added weight, and a standard D3 with a gallon of fuel in the tank now tipped the scales at 228lb, which could explain why it accelerated slightly less quickly than the plunger Major tested by T*he Motor Cycle* two years earlier.

The Telegram Bantams

If there's one role everyone of a certain age associates with the Bantam, apart from that of learner bike, first bike and everyday commuter, it's the GPO telegram bike. Cheap, light and easy to ride, it was ideal for the job, and within months of the Bantam's launch it had become the GPO's standard issue message machine, and would remain so up to the mid-1960s.

The Post Office didn't make widespread use of solo motorcycles until the 1930s, when its fleet of sidecar outfits was gradually replaced by small Morris vans, while solos were used for the rapidly expanding telegram delivery service. Telegrams weren't cheap, but they were the fastest means of sending a written message, and usually reserved for special occasions like births. The telegram

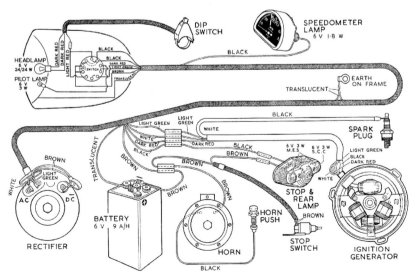

Even with battery lights, the wiring wasn't over-complex. (Billy Simpkins)

THE RIDE HOME

Subtitled *Mystery of a Recalcitrant Bantam, or What the Policeman Never Knew*, this story was written by one E M Clavey, and appeared in *The Motor Cycle* in October 1954. Miss Clavey had been out with Peter that evening, and when the time came to ride home, they mounted their respective machines and started home. After two miles their ways parted, and Miss Clavey – let's call her Emily – carried on, until her Bantam lost power ... and stopped.

"I started talking to the one-two-five. 'Binkie', I said, for that is his name, 'you can't do this to me.' There was no answer. 'Not to me, your ever-loving owner,' I wheedled. A hopeful jab at the kickstarter, a fiddle with the carburettor, and a few more kicks – still silence.'"

It was a black night with no moon, and Binkie had direct lighting, so no help there. Emily knew there was a house about 15 minutes' walk away, so she started pushing, and 20 minutes later she arrived. With her emergency lamp shining on the engine, she got to work. "Very knowingly, and copying every movement I had seen Peter make on a similar occasion, I carefully checked the plug – no excess gap or surplus dirt."

She had just put the plug back in when a young man from the house, probably alerted by the tinkling of spanners, emerged, listened to Emily's tale of woe, and unscrewed the plug. "I didn't protest, as I knew I might well have missed some important detail. He gazed at the plug, rubbed it on his sleeve, pronounced it fit, put it back, and swung the kickstarter expectantly ... never a murmur."

Then "a car zoomed past, nearly making scrap iron of Binkie and an awful mess of me. It screeched to a standstill some yards further on, backed and stopped, and six men climbed out." After asking a few questions, one unscrewed the plug, bathed it in a petrol-soaked handkerchief and screwed it back in. "The starter was duly kicked and 10 people sighed at the total non-response (by then the young man's parents had joined us at the gate)."

Two or three minutes passed before a policeman turned up on a 350 Ariel. "For one horrid moment I thought he was going to start on the sparking plug, but the authoritative gentleman from the car soon put him wise to the fact that 'that had been tried'." A quiet discussion between the two ensued before the policeman wondered if Emily had turned the fuel on.

"I was on the right side of Binkie for the petrol tap; I lowered my hand onto it – very casually, as if it was such a waste of time. 'Of course I have,' I said, at the same time giving the knob a sharp turn."

The policeman decided to try a bump-start "and the engine fairly burst into life, shattering the peace of the countryside. Everyone talked and joked and congratulated the policeman ... The next morning, when I stood before Matron on a charge of entering the hospital through a cloakroom window during the early hours, the incident was not at all amusing."

boys were invariably aged 16, dressed in a smart blue uniform and ... well, they were 16-year-old lads riding someone else's bike, and their ragged riding styles became the stuff of legends. "I used to watch the little buggers racing out of the main sorting office," recalled one ex-GPO worker. "There was a roundabout near the entrance, and they had this little game to see who could make the most sparks by grounding the footrests!"

BSA already made the telegram solo of choice before the Bantam arrived, usually as the 250cc C10, but when the GPO took delivery of its first Bantams in December 1948, it soon realised that this was the ideal telegram machine. The year before, it had experimented with autocycles, but the Bantam proved preferable.

It wasn't quite standard. The GPO specified a 30mph restrictor (though some more enterprising telegram boys soon found there were ways round this) and a 70mph speedo in place of the standard 55mph job – if there was a logic to that, it was known only to the GPO's top bureaucrats. The GPO-spec Bantam also came with legshields, parcel rack and canvas panniers, and every detail was checked at the factory by stern-faced GPO inspectors, right down to the length of the pannier straps. The first batch of Telegram Bantams was in the standard Mist Green, but the GPO soon specified proper Post Office red, complete with gold GPO decals on the legshields, a specific serial number and instead of a BSA badge on the tank, the royal seal.

Telegram Bantams might have been hard-used, but they had a full overhaul at a GPO depot every 15,000 miles, and were pensioned off after between five and seven years of service.

The Post Office bought thousands of Bantams. (Peter Henshaw)

One of the final Post Office Bantams, a B175. (Peter Henshaw)

Telegram Bantams came with legshields and splendid paintwork. (Peter Henshaw)

They look very different, but these early and late GPO Bantams shared a great deal.
(Peter Henshaw)

Even in the mid-60s, as telegram use began to decline as the telephone spread, the Post Office kept on buying Bantams. In all, it ordered 6574, most of which were plunger D1s, and GPO orders were what kept the basic 123cc D1 in production for so long. The last GPO D1 wasn't registered until September 1965, two years after BSA stopped making them

With the D1 no longer available, the GPO ordered D7s, then D10s and a final batch of B175s, though all in far fewer numbers than the D1, simply because the telegram service itself was winding down. The last Bantams were delivered to the Post Office in 1971, but some didn't enter service until 1974. When the telegram service was finally closed in 1982, the last pair of Bantams, both based in Sunderland, was pensioned off as well. The GPO's attachment to the Bantam wasn't simply down to blind faith – it had tried alternatives, but none measured up to the little red 125s in their heyday. In the '60s though, there were signs of a change. The licence laws changed, and 16-year-olds were restricted to mopeds, so the Post Office began to use Raleigh Runabouts and Supermatics as well as the Bantam, and tried other makes of moped in 1970/71, including Honda, Puch and Mobylette.

But the Telegram Bantam had already carved its place in the heart of the nation. Well, maybe that's over the top, but certainly among Bantam enthusiasts today, special reverence is reserved for any all-red GPO Bantam that survived countless miles delivering news of a birth, death or promotion, not to mention the tender care that only a succession 16-year-olds can inflict!

MY FIRST BANTAM – JOANIE

Long, long ago in the wild Northern Pennines, I had a friend who had a Bantam. I was about 14 at the time, and spent most of my time on horseback, but he taught me how to ride the bike, and I rode it successfully up a steep cindery hill, not changing gears too much, I think ... it was a long time ago. Many years later, and having passed my test on another bike, I was lucky enough to have the fun of riding a Triumph Trophy 650. Then there was another long gap until I bought my Bantam. It was an ex-GPO bike owned by my GP. I am not a mechanic, and the restoration was only possible because my partner agreed to do the work. It took a year, but I did ride the Banty, and had fun with it as my means of transport or just out for a run.
Then I went to live in Australia for six years. Three different friends looked after the Bantam in the meantime, and when I came back, a contact through the VMCC got it going again for me. I spent a few hundred pounds getting it sorted, until one day I was in the square at Marazion, and could not get it started again, it was completely dead. It went from person to person until someone had the time to find out what was wrong. The projected cost of repairs was well over £200, and as I could not afford that, and had nowhere to store it, I gave it to the chap in exchange for the work he had already done.
I still bitterly regret doing that, but I felt compelled to do it at the time, and did hold a secret hope that when I was recovered financially I would buy Banty back. It was not to be, as I heard from the chap later that he sold it as a project to someone else. Sad, innit? If I could re-run the film I would enrol on a Bantam mechanics course and rebuild the bike on the kitchen table. Hmm ... You're never too old to think outside the box, it just takes some of us a long time for the penny to drop.

Summary of GPO BSA Bantam purchases (copyright Post Office Vehicle Club 2001)

Serial number	Registration	Frame number	Engine number	Registration date
D1 rigid				
T1787-T1836	JYY 934-983	YD1 7051-7100		Dec 1948
T1837-T1886	KGO 1-50	YD1 10001-10050	YD1 5631-5680	Mar-Apr 1949
T1889-T1988	JXY 180-279	YD1 122001-122100		Dec 1949
T1989-T2088	JXY 830-929	YD1 122101-122200		Jan 1950
T2186-T2659	KYT 526-999	YD1 122201-122674		Dec '50-Apr 1951
T2660	LUU 564	YD1 122675		Apr 1951
D1 plunger				
T2664-T3002	MLH 54-392	YD1S 75000-75338	YD 122811-123149	Mar 1952
T3003-T3267	MYF 493-757	YD1S 83000-83264	YD 123150-123414	Oct 1952
T3268-T3367	NGJ 502-601	BD2S 10001-10100	BD2 5001-5100	Sept 1953
T3368-T3467	NGJ 602-701	BD2S 10101-10200	BDB 5101-5200	Oct 1953
T3468-T3627	PGO 668-827	BD2S 40001-40160	BDB 5201-5360	Jan 1955
T3628-T3927	RLB 160-459	BD2S 55001-55300	DDB 5362-5661	Sep/Oct 1955
T3928-T4146	RXT 661-879	BD2S 60000-60218	DDB 5662-5880	Jan-Apr 1956
T4147-T4526	SLO 583-962	BD2S 60219-60598	DDB 5881-6260	Jun/Jul 1956
T4527-T4542	TGC 274-289	BD2S 61492-61507	DDB 6271-6286	Oct 1956
T4543-T4649	TGC 893-999	BD2S 63000-63106	DDB 7001-7107	Sept 1957
T4650-T4692	TUV 1-43	BD2S 63107-63149	DDB 7108-7150	Sept 1957
T4693-T4742	TUV 912-961	BD2S 66000-66049	DDB 8301-8350	Mar 1958
T4743-T4792	UXH 921-970	BD2S 66050-66099	DDB 10101-10150	Mar 1958
T4793-T4942	UXV 100-249	BD2S 66100-66249	DDB 10151-10300	Mar&Jun 1958
T4943-T5002	UXV 250-309	BD2S 66601-66660	DDB 10311-10370	Jun 1958
T5003-T5263	WLA 327-587	BD2S 69000-69260	DDB 11401-11661	Mar 1959
T5264-T5529	YLH 101-366	BD2S 72001-72266	DDB 13251-13516	Apr 1960
T5530-T5904	1-375 BXE	BD2S 75000-75374	DDB 15201-15575	Mar 1961
T5911-T5999	682-770 DLF	BD2S 78001-78089	DDB 17001-17089	May 1962
T14000-T14228	771-999 DLF	BD2S 78090-78318	DDB 17090-17318	May-Jul 1962
T14229-T14255	1-27 DXV	BD2S 78319-78345	DDB 1739-17345	Jul 1962
T14284-T14317	966-999 FXY	BD2S 81000-81033	DDB 18514-18547	Oct 1963
T14318-T14538	715-980 FYM	BD2S 81034-81299	DDB 18548-18813	Oct-Dec 1963
T14584-T14933	ALC 1-350B	BD2S 81301-81650	DDB 18814-19163	Jun/Jul 1964
T14934-T15090	GLE 843-999C	BD2S 82001-82157	DDB 19201-19357	Sept 1965
T15091-T15308	GLU 1-218C	BD2S 82158-82375	DDB 19358-19575	Sept 1965
D7				
T15327-T15526	KVB 757-956D	HD7 101-300	HD7 101-300	Dec 1966
D10				
T15578-T15742	SYM 494-658F	BD10 101-265	BD10 101-265	Dec 1967
T15743-T15842	SLU 840-939F	BD10 266-365	BD10 266-365	Jul 1968
T15844-T15963	Locally registered	JCO 3001-3120	3001-3120	1969/1970
B175				
T282860-T282959	Locally registered	JCO 5001-5100	ADO 50015100	1970
T283085-T283484	Locally registered (prefix XD, AE or BE)	JCO 7101-7500	07101-07500	1970-73

Why not visit Veloce on the web? – www.velocebooks.com
New book news • Special offers • Details of all books in print • Gift vouchers

37

D5: Super Bantam

4

The D5 – building the Bantam

"When is the Bantam gonna stop growing?" That was the reaction of a Canadian reader of *The Motor Cycle* to BSA's launch of the 174cc Bantam in December 1957. He might well ask, though as it happened, this was the last stretch for the Bantam, which would stick at 174cc for the rest of its production life.

The Bantam Major, it transpired, wasn't enough. Not only was the power increase fairly modest, but in the process it had lost some of the easy-going character of the original D1. The Major was a whole lot heavier too, thanks to beefier forks and engine internals, plus from 1956 the swingarm rear end. So the end result was only slightly better performance, which didn't really have the oomph to carry a pillion, certainly on main roads or for long distances, and with a dual seat now standard,

Bantam owners quite reasonably assumed that two-up performance was part of the package. Hence the 174cc D5, which was intended to boost the Bantam's performance up to that of the rival two-strokes powered by the ubiquitous Villiers 197. Actually, BSA's first attempt was a long-stroke version of the Bantam engine, matching the Villiers' 197cc capacity, with dimensions of 57 x 72mm. It certainly had the required power, and its torque was sufficient to destroy the chain adjusters, but it also had fearsome vibration, thanks to extremely heavy flywheels.

In the end, the BSA design team (now moved from Redditch to company HQ at Small Heath) found a much simpler route to more power. Increasing the bore to 61.5mm and leaving the stroke at 58mm brought 174cc, which, with an increase in compression ratio to 7.4:1, was enough to deliver the extra horsepower without making too many changes to the rest of the bike. The team have to move the crankcase studs out to 60mm, to make room for the bigger bore, so as with the 148cc Major, it wasn't possible to fit this bigger barrel to an earlier crankcase. Sensibly, they also took the opportunity to strengthen the big-end. Bigger rollers, 4mm in diameter and 8mm long, were held in place in duralumin half-cages – all previous Bantam big-ends were uncaged – while lubrication was improved by radial oilways feeding into the big-end. To make the most of the cubic capacity, a bigger 7/8in Amal carburettor was

This is a D3, but the D5 used the same swingarm frame with smaller 18-inch wheels. (Roger Fogg)

38

175 c.c. model D5
BANTAM SUPER

The Bantam Super now added to the B.S.A. range has a 175 c.c. engine, swinging-arm rear suspension, a new 2 gallon petrol tank, and a smart maroon finish. With its powerful engine and larger brakes this is a machine now even better equipped to perform the long distance tours so frequently undertaken by Bantam owners.

Shefford,
Bedfordshire

'Now even better-equipped to perform the long-distance tours so frequently undertaken by Bantam owners.' (Peter Old)

added as well, and to ensure that the clutch didn't complain about the extra power, the old cork insert plates were ditched in favour of bonded-on Neolangite-faced plates.

The end result of all this beefing and upgrading was a substantial power increase to 7.5bhp, or put another way, 44 per cent more than the 148cc Bantam Major. According to *The Motor Cycle*'s road test, the new D5 Bantam Super weighed no more than the old one, and so it was faster. Here was a Bantam that could virtually top 60mph, cruise at 55mph and didn't baulk too much at the extra poundage of a passenger.

The D3 Major's brakes would have been hard pushed to keep up with this sort of performance, so the width (front and rear) was increased by ¼in to ⅞in. Still not wonderful, and the Bantam's big step forward in braking would have to wait for the next year's D7, but it was at least an improvement.

SURTEES THE BANTAMITE!
John Surtees, before achieving worldwide fame on the race track, served an apprenticeship with Vincent-HRD. He was sometimes lent one of the ultimate V-twins to ride home on test, but, commuting between Stevenage and his parents' house in Forest Hill, he found that his mother's Bantam was quicker through London traffic. Still, his Bantam-riding era didn't last long, and he soon went on to bigger (but not necessarily better) things. "By the time I was 18 I was picking up enough prize money to be able to afford a 1½-litre Jowett Jupiter two-seater sports car," he later recalled. Bet it wasn't as quick across town as mum's Bantam though.

The D5 Super briefly retained the same 'Major' tag as its predecessor, but the marketing men soon had a change of heart – an increasingly affluent country was heading headlong into the flash, chrome-plated, rocketship age of 'Super'. 'Major' was somehow tweedier and more comfortable, but not exactly exciting. Bantam Super it was then.

Despite the new name, the Major's frame and cycle parts mostly carried on unchanged, though there was a fatter two-gallon fuel tank and bigger triangular side panels. It was the first sign that BSA was attempting to trade on the Bantam's big bike looks, though some thought it had gone too far, and that the effect gave the impression of middle-aged flab rather than a miniature A10 Golden Flash. Smaller 18in wheels were part of the package, though these would have had the effect of lowering overall gearing slightly. To compensate, BSA upped the ratios of the three-speed gearbox, fitted a one-tooth-bigger gearbox sprocket (now 16T) and a one-tooth-smaller rear sprocket (46T). There were a few other minor changes, including the fork internals, while C10 handlebars were fitted.

Electrics were still based around the Wico-Pacy flywheel magneto, still with the choice of direct lighting or, for those who could afford the extra few pounds, rectifier and battery lighting. Colours were still sober rather than flash, with a choice of Bayard Crimson (a sort of maroon) or black, both with an ivory tank panel. The tank badge gained a 'Bantam Super' script, with its cockerel crowing more proudly than ever.

BSA often featured women in Bantam adverts, because it was targeting female riders. (Peter Old)

A nicely kept, but not over-restored, D3 Major. (Roger Fogg)

The press

The Motor Cycle tested a rectifier-and-battery D5 in March 1958, this particular one fitted with the optional legshields and windscreen. The legshields cost £2 1s 2d extra, and the screen (named 'Bantam Major') £2 13s, not much to ask for substantially better weather protection, and just the thing for touring or all-year round commuting.

All of these accessories were made by Motoplas, a wholly-owned BSA subsidiary formerly known as the Motor Plastic Company. As well as making original equipment for the BSAs – things like seats, tyre pumps and licence holders – Motoplas also offered them as aftermarket accessories for upgrading an existing bike.

By the mid-60s the Bantam range included the big Tri-point screen, legshields (now made of glassfibre, not steel) and panniers, the latter costing £9 5s 4d a pair. There was also a choice

For the D5, the little two-stroke would be stretched to its biggest size yet. (Roger Fogg)

The new engine added useful performance to the Bantam, but was still hampered by the wide-ratio, three-speed gearbox. (Roger Fogg)

of mirrors. The stainless-steel backed Monsoon Continental cost 17s 9d, though a pair came as part of the deal on the Bantam Supreme. A more affordable alternative cost 13s 6d, with, 'a colourful PVC head', and went by the name of 'Gay-Plas'. Ah, innocent days. Well, they weren't at all that innocent, of course, it's just that language has changed in the meantime.

So what did *The Motor Cycle* think of the Motoplas-equipped Bantam Super? The legshields came in for particular praise. With no overboots or leggings, the tester claimed to have ridden to work through a heavy downpour, with "only a few rain spots" reaching his shoes and trousers. The Bantam Major screen was thought rather narrow, but still very effective in protecting the chest and face. It was tall by the standards of modern screens, with an adjustable visor clipped to the top, giving a little slit to peer through if it was raining.

The Super couldn't quite crack 60mph, even after the screen was removed and the rider crouched into the wind, with a best one-way of 59mph and an average top speed of 57mph. Mind you, that was with a strong crosswind and the rider "bulkily clad" which in those days meant a massive two-piece wax cotton Belstaff which did no favours for aerodynamic effectiveness. So on a still day with a leather-jacketed pilot, nose on the tank, maybe a true 60mph really was possible.

The test told of cruising at near maximum speed: "One undulating main road run of over 30 miles was accomplished with the speedometer needle held near the 60s for almost the whole distance," which sounded impressive, but given

MY FIRST BANTAM – PETE KELLY
"I owned a 150 Bantam that I fitted a racing seat and tank to, Belco-brushed it green and cream, cleaned the ports, chopped the exhaust, removed the baffles, found a Dura-Glit tin lid, punched a load of holes in it, painted it red and fitted it over the end. I can't remember whether I also went for a Norton spark enhancer. Anyway, my mods made the bike go a good 5mph slower and it was useless on hills, but you could hear it from two miles away!"

a speedo over-reading by 10 per cent meant a realistic 52-53mph. Still, it was streets ahead of any previous Bantam, and even with the addition of a heavy passenger, "the model was still able to accelerate smartly from rest and hold its own in the traffic stream." That combined rider and pillion weight of nearly 400lb also made the rear shocks bottom out on poor surfaces, but you couldn't have everything.

The extra cubic capacity also appeared to have regained the Bantam's tractability, and the Super could trickle along at 20mph in top, and pull away without faltering (though not very quickly). Road manners were "exemplary" (even on frozen snow, according to the brave tester) and vibration was "at no time noticeable." But there was one

Small Heath might well have the know-how, but would management give it free rein? (Roger Fogg)

Bantam characteristic that even 1950s testers felt compelled to criticise: when working hard, the Super's exhaust note was "decidedly raucous".

Building the Bantam

From the start, Bantam engines were built at Redditch, but the complete bikes were assembled at the giant Small Heath plant. Just like the Bantam, the Redditch factory on Studley Road was a spoil of war. It was a satellite plant, built to keep up with the massive demand for munitions during World War II, and in particular to make the BESA machine gun. BSA of course, stood for Birmingham Small Arms, and the company started out as a group of Birmingham gunsmiths in 1861.

By the end of World War II, the company employed 28,000 people, and the Redditch plant alone had massive capacity, with its own foundries and machine shops. So it made plenty of things besides the Bantam power unit, including industrial engines and the Sunbeam S7, that civilised but low-powered shaft-drive in-line twin that BSA hoped would fill a niche as a gentleman's machine, just like the original flat-tank Sunbeams. The S7 certainly looked classy, in the same Mist Green as the D1 Bantam (its assembly line was next to that for Bantam engines), but most motorcyclists preferred the cheaper, faster pushrod alternatives from Triumph, Norton and BSA itself. Towards the end of production, only a handful of S7s were being turned out each week.

Studley Road's Bantam operation was a great success, with anything between 90 and 125 engine/gearbox units produced every day. On the assembly track, two rows of men faced each other, each man doing a single job before sliding the engine along to the next man. When the engines were finished, they were inspected and stamped with a number in batches, then shipped off to Small Heath.

Here, the final assembly of Bantams was carried out almost entirely by women; during both world wars, women were recruited into munitions production in large numbers, as the men were

When you buy a BSA motorcycle you buy BSA "Know-How"

Behind every BSA stands more than a hundred years of precision engineering experience—experience which ensures that your BSA is designed right down to the smallest detail to give you the performance, reliability and service which are automatically associated with the BSA name in every part of the world.

In the wide BSA range there is a model for every purse and purpose—be it work, play or sport—from the little 75 cc. Beagle to the exciting new ultra high performance Cyclone and Lightning twins.

Whatever your need, you can find a BSA which will serve you better than anything else.

See your local BSA dealer, examine the models he has in his showroom—ask his advice, he is there to help you—choose BSA, today.

THE END OF THE LINE
Thousands of complex machine tools have completed hundreds of thousands of intricate operations to produce the parts of a motorcycle which have come together for the first time on the assembly track and are swiftly built into complete machines. From the end of this track experienced and hard-to-please testers check every detail, test ride, re-check and then, if satisfied pass them off for despatch to the far corners of the world.

SEWING UP THE FRAME !
Here is a "sewing machine" with a difference—it sews, or to be more precise, it welds the two halves of the Beagle pressed steel chassis together, down the seams—at 3 ft. per minute ! Another precision operation typical of BSA manufacture.

The D5 was the last Bantam to have that distinctive D-shaped speedo. (Roger Fogg)

called up to fight. The dexterity and patience of female labour made management realise that here was a workforce well suited to assembly work. BSA found women were more consistently accurate than men, and in those days they were cheap, often paid only half as much for doing the same

This story starts with a letter arriving in Birmingham, about ten years after the factory at Small Heath was demolished, addressed to "BSA Motorcycles, Armoury Road, Small Heath", with an Argentinian postmark. It was taken to a local museum, where it was opened and discovered to be from an Argentinian farmer. He had bought a brand new D1 Bantam in the early 1950s, but now his kickstart ratchet assembly was worn out.

So he did what any other owner would do, looked up BSA's address in the handbook and wrote ordering a new one. What to do? The museum passed his request on to a BSA Owners Club member, who handed it to the club's national committee. They sent the farmer a new kickstart assembly free of charge, along with life membership of the BSAOC.

The farmer was so chuffed that when he learnt of a BSAOC rally in California a year or two later, he rode up from Argentina on his D1. The journey took a month, but he met up with the national committee, thanked them for their generosity and the next day, set off back home to Argentina.

Happiness is ... a nicely repainted Bantam. (Roger Fogg)

job. It was scandalous, but it was the way things were – BSA wasn't alone in underpaying women workers, who did almost everything on the Bantam from wheel-building to wiring and frame assembly.

THE OTHER BANTAM
BSA's wasn't the first two-wheeled Bantam. Douglas built one in the 1930s. It was a 150cc two-stroke, using Douglas' own engine, launched in 1933. With a tubular steel frame and Albion three-speed gearbox, it was initially named the Snowden, but that never caught on. So, the Douglas Bantam it was.

As each Bantam was finished, it was wheeled into a holding area before being given a half-mile test run around Small Heath's test track. According to John Cox, who worked at Small Heath between 1950 and 1956, this was intended to test engine and transmission "at both extremities of twist grip travel"! In later years, probably to the delight of testers in winter, but their despair in summer, this outdoor life was superseded by an indoor rolling road. If all was well, the bike was sent to the despatch bay to await shipping to a BSA dealer at home or abroad. Another brand new Bantam had found its owner.

Why not visit Veloce on the web? – www.velocebooks.com
New book news • Special offers • Details of all books in print • Gift vouchers

43

WORKSHOP MEMORIES – BILLY SIMPKINS

Billy Simpkins lived in Cornwall all his life and worked on lots of bikes, Bantams among them.
"The D1 was tougher than the later ones, I think – the coil ignition ones had more to go wrong. A friend of mine, Roger Thorn from Surrey, used to ride down to Cornwall on his, and he was a big chap. I used to call the D14 'self-exploding'.

"I can remember lots of odd things with them, like the pin holding the points plate on, which could come loose. The cure was to open up the hole with a centre punch then swage the pin back in.

"I came across two girls one day whose Bantam had just stopped and wouldn't restart. I realised that there was an air leak behind the barrel. Did they have any nail varnish? Yes they did, so I painted some of that over the leak, and the bike started! I don't know if they ever got home.

"Bantams were so variable. I saw one D3 that started well but then died and simply would not run. It turned out to have a tiny leak through a crank seal. Then there was another that was running quite happily, though there was a strange fluffing noise. The crankcase drain plug was missing altogether, yet the bike was still running!

"Mains wear would put the points out of adjustment until the bike would four-stroke. The answer (apart from renewing the bearings) was to just tighten the points until the engine ran well – that would get you home. Revving hard could also pull the points open. Bulbs could blow on direct lighting at high revs too – fitting a little diode prevented that.

"Flywheel compression discs were peened sheet steel, and could come loose then would carry on spinning for about fifteen seconds after the engine stopped, and you'd hear this faint tsk-tsk-tsk. I used fibreglass to keep them in place.

"Although they varied, there were no lemons – it was a darn good little bike."

5

D7: was bigger better?

Middle-aged spread – American Dream – the Tiger Cub connection

The D7, as far as most Bantamites are concerned, was a real break with the past. True, it used exactly the same 174cc engine as the D5, and the gearbox remained that wide-ratio three-speeder, but the philosophy had changed. The Bantam was restyled to make it look even more like a big bike, but somehow this didn't work. From the very first D1, one of the BSA's strengths was that it looked like a proper motorbike, not some overgrown autocycle or moped. But it was still obviously a handsome lightweight, with everything in proportion. The D7, in the eyes of many, lost that lightweight feel,

looking as if it had become flabby and middle aged.

In the words of Barry Ryerson, "The Bantam continued to develop until, at least in the eyes of the experts, it outgrew its own strength and lost the simplicity which had been the very foundation of its success." And, today, plenty of Bantam enthusiasts still much prefer the basic D1 to the later fully-equipped and flashy 175. But was a rigid D1, however charming its simplicity, a realistic alternative to a Honda? The answer was 'of course not', and BSA had no choice but to update the Bantam. The problem wasn't that it updated it too much, but not enough, and the D7 was hardly changed in seven years of production. At a time when Honda and Suzuki lightweights were starting to make inroads into the UK (and just as significant for BSA at the time, the USA) market, the Bantam was standing still. These bikes had indicators and pumped lubrication – on a Bantam, you mixed the petroil yourself and relied on hand signals.

But a few years earlier, in 1959, the threat to lightweight motorcycle sales came from Italy. This was the height of the scooter boom, and of the 330,000 two-wheelers registered in Britain, over half were scooters. Vespa and Lambretta – stylish, cool and convenient – had shown the way, and British manufacturers were struggling to catch up with scooters of their own. In Germany, buyers had deserted two wheels altogether for a small car, but over the Channel the public still bought two-

The D7 Super with optional chrome panels looks a very different bike to the little red D1. (Peter Old)

45

Freshly restored D7 – the bulbous side panels and valanced mudguards were following fashions of the time. (Roger Fogg)

wheelers in large numbers to ride to work on. The difference now was that many of them didn't want to be bothered by greasy chains and exposed oily engines. Bigger bikes were caught up in the fashion too, and even the rip-roaring Triumphs acquired extra bodywork in the style of the times.

BSA thought it had no choice but to follow suit, launching the clean looking unit construction C15, one class above the Bantam. Complete with valanced mudguards and a headlamp nacelle, the latest 250 BSA showed the way things were going, and BSA's twins went unit construction a couple of years later. And of course, this all trickled down to the Bantam.

The new look

The new Bantam D7 Super looked quite different to the D5, but instead of going down the enclosure route, it concentrated on details. There was a new frame, with cleaner rear end styling and neater, more rounded side panels, joined by a panel that hid the frame's rear downtube. The panels looked

neat, but refitting their hollow retaining screws onto the hidden threads behind the cover was a frustrating and linguistically colourful business. Talking of colour, instead of the subtle but dowdy old greys, greens and maroons, the D7 came in Royal Red, a bright and cheerful shade that was a real departure by Bantam standards.

The seat was carefully styled to blend in with the clean and simple look, while the headlamp was part of a streamlined nacelle that met the fork top cover. The nacelle contained the lighting switch and a round speedometer, which meant the original Bantam's D-shaped Smiths speedo was finally consigned to history. Valanced mudguards hadn't been seen since the early D1, but now they were back, albeit in a smoother, more elegant form.

The engine/gearbox got the same treatment, with a one-piece cover on the generator side to give the unit an all-in-one symmetrical appearance. To complete the transformation, and to underline just how super the new Bantam

Better looks Better performance Better features

a new **BSA** 175 cc

Bantam Super

Go to work on an egg? A D7 Bantam would be a better bet.

was, a curly 'Super' script was emblazoned over the new cover. From the start, the Bantam engine had been described as a 'power egg' – now it looked like one too. So the adverts put out by the Egg Marketing Board, starring Tony Hancock, were absolutely bang on when applied to a nation of Bantam riders. Hadn't Tony exhorted them to "Go to work on an Egg"?

Anyway, it wasn't all about styling. New hydraulically-damped forks were shorter versions of the Triumph Tiger Cub, holding C15 steering head bearings. It had taken the Bantam more than ten years to graduate from its simple greased forks with a rubber damper, but it had finally got there. The swingarm changed as well, ditching the Metalastic rubber bushes in favour of bronze items. These were an improvement, giving more positive rear wheel location ... as long as they were kept well-greased. Even then, there was a tendency for tiny parts of the case hardened spindle to break off and become embedded in the bronze bush,

The D7 was bigger all round than its predecessors. (Roger Fogg)

47

which then wore out in double-quick time. If the owner didn't recognise the increasing play in the swingarm, they could end up with a form of rear wheel steering!

The brakes were updated too, but here the news was all good. The old pressed-steel hubs were swapped for cast-iron ones, and BSA also increased the drum size, putting half an inch on the diameter and upping the shoe width to a full inch. For the first time, a Bantam had brakes that were better than adequate. There was a consensus that the new frame handled well, and backed up by the hydraulic forks, bronze-bushed swingarm and decent brakes, gave the Bantam a dynamically respectable chassis. Everyone agreed, too, that the D7 motor was very pleasant. It was tractable and torquey, quite laid-back for a two-stroke, and if it didn't have the thump of a Tiger Cub, it certainly had less to go wrong and was more tolerant of abuse. Today, some still prefer these characteristics to the peppier, fussier high-compression four-speed Bantams that followed.

If there was a flaw in all of this, it was the gearbox. As ever, having three widely-spaced ratios was a bit of a nuisance, especially on hills where you had the choice of slogging the engine in top, or screaming it in second. But that was part of the Bantam experience, and most accepted it as such. The D7's specific problem lay with the mainshaft and layshaft. An extra set of splines had previously been added, but these were now deleted again, to save money – without the extra splines, the shafts didn't need to be hollow, which made them simpler and cheaper to make. The trouble was, the gearbox ended up weaker than the original D1 box, but with double the power to cope with. The result was stripped gears or jumping out of second, though the D7 did include a modification to the selector to try and eliminate this long-standing problem. Finally (though this was an engine rather than a gearbox problem) the D7's crankshaft could snap at the Woodruff key, partly because of the 175's extra power, partly because BSA had increased the width of the key without doing the same for the crank.

After the storm ...

After so many momentous changes, the Bantam was left alone for a few years, and the changes were mostly cosmetic. For 1960, the D1 cycle parts were finished in black and the D7 had a lug added to the frame for padlocking the steering. The following year, the D7 said farewell to the rooster tank transfers that in one form or another had graced almost every Bantam since the D1. In their place were big BSA star badges, moving

Not a standard colour, but with so many D7s around, who's going to complain? (Roger Fogg)

the Bantam into line with the rest of the range. And as if Royal Red wasn't enough, Sapphire Blue joined the colour choices, with the new option of a chrome side panel on the tank, lined in gold. The Flash Harry Bantam hadn't quite arrived yet, but he was on his way.

There were a few technical changes. For 1962, the small-end bearing became a Torrington needle race, which was an improvement, and the gearbox splines were modified, but didn't return to their stronger form, which wasn't. And the gearing was marginally lowered by fitting a 47T rear sprocket.

Motorcycling tested a Sapphire Blue D7 in the winter of 1962 (that was early '62, not the legendary snow season that came later in the year). The Bantam was resplendent with its optional chrome tank panel, but behind the glitz, there were signs that it was falling behind. For the first time, road tests observed that the Bantam was unusual for a lightweight, being lower-revving (it peaked at 5000rpm) and slower than its rivals. Of course, they were quick to point out that the upside was its torquey, tractable nature, but it was quite different to reaction to that for the willing

'A gratifying range of road performance,' all for £122 14s 9d. (Peter Old)

little D1. In fact, the D7 actually proved slower than the D5. Road tests quoted an average top speed of 54mph and an extra couple of seconds to cover a standing quarter-mile. They weren't big differences, but not the way to go when peppier, revvier rivals were coming onto the market.

Still, there were evidently people around who liked these characteristics. Veteran tester Bob Currie, later on record as preferring the low-revving three-speed D7 to the peakier D10 and D14 that followed it, rode one for *The Motor Cycle* in 1964, and loved it. To him the Bantam was "an endearingly flexible little mount with boundless energy in the lower reaches of the scale."

He reckoned 27 stone of passenger and rider gave performance little short of solo riding, but echoed the *The Motor Cycle* criticism of stiff rear shocks when riding one-up. It also had a light gearchange and clutch, and like the very early Bantams, a surprising ability off-road. And while the D7 Super might be the heaviest Bantam yet, at 232lb with a gallon of petroil in the tank, it still didn't use much fuel. Bob's test recorded 136mpg at a steady 30mph, and more than 90mpg overall – *Motorcycling*'s unnamed tester made it 97mpg.

175 BANTAM SUPER MODEL D7

Chrome tank panels as illustrated £3. 10s. extra.

The Bantam Super has a 175 cc engine, and its telescopic forks and swinging-arm rear suspension are both hydraulically damped. The headlamp nacelle and two gallon tank of modern design, together with the attractive colour schemes of Royal red or Sapphire blue and new dome section mudguards contribute to its handsome appearance, while its more powerful engine and larger brakes provide a gratifying range of road performance.

Engine. D1—123 cc (52 × 58 mm.), D7—173 cc (61.5 × 58 mm.), single cylinder two-stroke; caged roller bearing big-end; timing side supported by ball race, drive-side by two ball races; positive oil feed to main bearings; petroil lubrication; silencer with detachable baffle unit.

Carburettor. Amal with twist grip throttle control; Monobloc type on D7; air cleaner.

Transmission. B.S.A. 3-speed gearbox with positive-stop foot control, built in unit construction with engine; gear ratios D1, 7.0—11.7—22.1; D7, 6.43—10.74—20.2; clutch with bonded resilient facings; primary chain ⅜ × .250" in oil-bath case; rear chain ½ × .335" with guard over top run.

Ignition and Lighting. Wico-Pacy flywheel generator with direct lighting; 6" diameter headlamp; bulb horn; illuminated speedometer. D7 has headlamp nacelle housing pre-focus headlight unit with pilot light, speedometer and switchgear. Battery lighting set with combined stop and tail lamp, electric horn and 8 amp. hr. battery extra.

Fuel Capacity. D1, 1¾ gallons; D7, 2 gallons.

Tyres. Dunlop reinforced lightweight 2.75—19 front and rear on D1; 3.00—18 on D7. Whitewall tyres, see extra fittings.

Brakes. 5" diameter, ⅞" wide on D1 and 5¼" diameter × 1" wide on D7. Finger-operated adjusters.

Direct Lighting	Battery Lighting
£122. 14s. 9d.	£125. 15s. 1d.
including £20. 19s. 9d. purchase tax	including £21. 10s. 1d. purchase tax

BSA did recognise that what the Bantam really needed was a four-speed gearbox, and indeed one had not only been designed, but was out on the road being tested by a young Chris Vincent, who had just won the International Sidecar TT for BSA. Sadly, the new four-speed cluster didn't stay in one place for long, and was full of false neutrals. The whole project was abandoned after Vincent and the four-speed D7 were hit by a large lorry – Vincent was fine, but there wasn't much left of the D7, which, according to author Owen Wright, was consigned to Small Heath's famous black hole, a burial reserved for experiments that didn't work. BSA had also been working on a separate oiling system for the Bantam, and by 1964 a prototype had apparently covered thousands of miles on the road. It was turned down by the management, for cost reasons.

American influence

The trouble was, there were reasons why BSA was apparently reluctant to spend real money on developing the Bantam in the early 1960s. The company was going through turbulent times, and, in fact, author Barry

Nicely kept, Fuschia Red D7 Super, with original paintwork. (Roger Fogg)

The BSA Bantam Bible

The D7 later came in Sapphire Blue, which didn't translate well on black and white brochures ... (Peter Old)

Ryerson thought that BSA had been in decline since the 1956 boardroom coup. Not all of this was down to mismanagement. In Britain, motorcycle sales slumped, which after the boom years of the late-'50s hit especially hard. BSA's strategy to cope with this was to follow its Triumph subsidiary in promoting heavily in the USA market.

North America had two things to recommend it for any motorcycle maker – it was a vast market, which was growing rapidly, and BSA took advantage. Its exports to the States were worth £1 million in 1964, and within two years had quadrupled. The company may have been export-driven in the early post-war years, but that had tailed off as it sought to satisfy a healthy home market. Now the tables were turned, and more than two-thirds of Small Heath's production was heading abroad, most of it to the USA. It must have seemed like a golden opportunity at the time, but this increasing dependence on America would bring in its own problems a few years later. In the meantime, BSA was earning oodles of hard currency, and it could bask in the glory of winning a Queen's Award for Exports two years running. In 1965/66, BSA/Triumph together exported more bikes by value than any British make of car – more than MG or Jaguar or Triumph sports cars, all of which famously made hay in North America at the time.

But where did all this leave the Bantam? The

A round speedometer, set into the headlight, was part of the new look. (Roger Fogg)

High-rise bars, lots of chrome, and 'Flash' in the name, but Americans still didn't take to the Bantam. (Peter Old)

Extra weight on the D7 began to tell on the 174cc engine's performance. (Roger Fogg)

THE NEW  BANTAM SUPER
175 c.c. model D7

ENGINE. Single cylinder two-stroke, 61.5 x 58 mm., 173 c.c. Caged roller big end. Double ball race drive-side mainshaft, single on flywheel side, all with positive oil feed. Petroil lubrication to other engine parts. Amal monobloc carburetter with air cleaner. Large capacity silencer with detachable baffle unit.

TRANSMISSION. Gearbox in unit construction with engine. Primary chain in oilbath compartment. Clutch with bonded resilient linings and three-speed gear with positive stop foot change. Gear ratios 6.43, 10.74, and 20.2.

FRAME. New design tubular cradle frame. Telescopic front forks with hydraulic damping. Hydraulically damped swinging arm rear suspension. Two gallon petrol tank. Deeply valanced mudguards. New design toolbox and battery carrier. Dunlop tyres 3.00 x 18. Brakes 5½″ dia. x 1″ wide. Adjustable footrests. Dual seat and pillion footrests.

ELECTRICAL EQUIPMENT. Wico-Pacy lighting set. New headlamp nacelle housing pre-focus headlight unit with pilot light, speedometer and switch gear. Battery set has combined stop and tail lamp and electric horn. Battery and horn housed in special compartment adjoining the new toolbox.

FINISH. Royal Red mudguards, toolbox and battery container, and petrol tank with cream panels and chrome strips. Frame and forks black. Chrome wheel rims, spokes, handlebars and other bright parts. Alternative colour black.

EXTRAS. Legshields, safety bars and prop stand.

In its attractive colour finish of Royal Red — you can still have black if you prefer — the D7 Bantam Super simply bristles with new features including redesigned frame with cradle-mounted dual seat, hydraulically damped front forks, larger and wider brakes, new style mudguards and other items of design which enhance the appeal of this most popular of lightweights.

Price with direct lighting ...	£126	18s.	8d.	(including £25	3s. 8d. P.T.)
Price with battery lighting ...	£130	1s.	1d.	(including £25	16s. 1d. P.T.)

B.S.A. MOTOR CYCLES LTD., BIRMINGHAM 11

B.S.A. Motor Cycles Ltd. Birmingham 11, England, reserve the right to alter designs or any constructional details of their manufactures at any time without giving notice.

It looked different, but the D7 Bantam was still a very simple machine. (Peter Old)

Plain black D7, awaiting a new owner. (Roger Fogg)

answer was not in the healthy state it had been through the 1950s. The Americans wanted big, sporty twins from the British, not little two-strokes. There were attempts to make the Bantam part of this US bonanza, but with its petroil lubrication and modest performance, it simply didn't fit in. In 1965, BSA sold just 56 US-spec Bantam Pastorals. It wasn't the sort of thing to encourage investment in a serious update. As Bert Hopwood pointed out in his book *Whatever Happened to the British Motorcycle Industry?*, petroil was just too messy, crude and inconvenient in America, especially an America just discovering the delights of a simple and clean little Honda on which one met the nicest people.

Meanwhile, UK sales continued in the doldrums, slumping by 31 per cent in 1965. With sales down at home, and refusing to take off in the States, Bantam production began to dwindle. In 1964 (before US sales really took off) BSA

At £106 14s 10d, the basic D1 was still the cheapest BSA you could buy in 1961.
(Peter Old)

built just over 18,000 bikes, and just over 3900 of them were Bantams. It sounds respectable, but wasn't much compared to the glory days of the D1. The Bantam was meant to be the mass-market, mass-seller of the BSA range, but the company sold more 650cc twins that year. Nearly 60,000 Lightnings and Thunderbolts were made between 1963 and 1972, but far fewer Bantams. In 1965/66 Bantam production had sunk so low that BSA could no longer justify the separate engine assembly line at Redditch – engine production was moved to Small Heath.

In short, the Bantam was fast becoming the Cinderella of the range. It's hardly surprising that for 1965 BSA didn't announce a four-speed Bantam, or one with a separate oil tank, but the D7 De Luxe instead. This was a purely cosmetic variation on the Super. Its highlight was a new 1.95-gallon fuel tank, the kidney shaped one that was fitted to almost every subsequent Bantam, with big chrome panels, knee indents and a circular BSA star badge. Ball-ended levers were part of the deal (to give some off-road credibility) and the new torpedo-shaped silencer had a black end cap

BSA MOTOR CYCLES

PRICE LIST FROM 26th JULY, 1961

Model	Price	Purchase Tax plus 10% Surcharge	Total
	£ s. d.	£ s. d.	£ s. d.
650 O.H.V. Twin A10 Super Rocket	227 0 0	51 10 1	278 10 1
650 O.H.V. Twin A10 Golden Flash	215 0 0	48 15 7	263 15 7
500 O.H.V. Twin A7 Shooting Star	217 5 0	49 5 9	266 10 9
500 O.H.V. Twin A7	211 10 0	47 19 9	259 9 9
500 O.H.V. B34 Gold Star Clubman's ...	259 5 0	58 16 4	318 1 4
500 O.H.V. B34 Gold Star Scrambles ...	230 15 0	52 7 1	283 2 1
600 S.V. M21	185 10 0	42 1 9	227 11 9
350 O.H.V. B40 Star	169 18 11	38 11 2	208 10 1
250 O.H.V. C15 Star	142 15 0	32 7 10	175 2 10
250 O.H.V. C15 Star Scrambles ...	149 5 0	33 17 3	183 2 3
250 O.H.V. C15 Star Trials ...	153 5 0	34 15 5	188 0 5
250 O.H.V. C15SS80 Sport Star (Chrome Guards)	160 0 0	36 6 0	196 6 0
175 D7 Bantam Super (Direct Lighting)... ...	101 15 0	23 1 9	124 16 9
175 D7 Bantam Super (Battery Lighting) ...	104 5 0	23 13 1	127 18 1
125 D1 Bantam (Direct Lighting)	87 0 0	19 14 10	106 14 10
125 D1 Bantam (Battery Lighting)	91 0 0	20 12 11	111 12 11

Prices are subject to alteration without notice. Prices charged will be those ruling at date of despatch.

MC 1306–50. July 26th, 1961.

B.S.A. Motor Cycles Ltd., Birmingham 11

without finning. And as if Royal Red wasn't radical enough, BSA now rocked the motorcycle world with Flamboyant Red. This was an early metallic, achieved by spraying plain red over a silver base, set off by white coach lining on the mudguards and red piping on the black dual seat, which had a grab handle.

It all worked rather well, for here was a Bantam transformed from a worthy Clement Atlee into a flamboyant George Brown. Mechanically, the De Luxe Bantam was identical to the Super, though it came in battery form only. If you insisted, the Super could still be had with basic direct lighting. Nor did BSA ask much for it; Bob Currie tested a De Luxe, and pointed out that at £141 all in, it was actually cheaper than the '64 Super.

The following year, the Super was dropped, replaced by an economy Bantam, the D7 Silver. This did without the De Luxe's chrome, its ball-ended levers and so on, but kept the new fuel tank, which was finished in Sapphire Blue, while the mudguards, headlamp cowl and tank side panels were in polychromatic silver. "The NEW Silver Bantam," went the adverts. "Lowest in price, sky-high in value. Penny-for-penny, mile-for-mile, the new Silver Bantam is unbeatable in the 175cc market."

So the D7 ended on a cheerful note, but after seven years of mostly cosmetic tweaking, the

Fuzzy picture, happy days – Morf from Cornwall, and a mate. (Morf)

The Bantam Cub made economic sense, although marque loyalists didn't agree. (Roger Fogg)

Bantam was about to finally get some substantial changes.

The Cub connection

History has not treated the Triumph Bantam Cub kindly, though it made perfect sense in terms of economics. Triumph's Meriden factory was struggling to meet demand for its big twins from the USA, so management consultants McKinseys recommended moving Tiger Cub production to Small Heath. At the same time, fitting the Tiger Cub with Bantam D7 frame and cycle parts would save a lot of money.

So that's exactly what BSA did, but the directors (and certainly McKinseys) hadn't reckoned on the strong feelings this would stir up. BSA had taken over Triumph back in 1951, but for the next decade or more, the two sides of the business were run virtually as separate companies. There was fierce brand loyalty, not just between Triumph and BSA owners, but between the dealers and the Meriden and Small Heath workers as well. Brand loyalty is a keen sales weapon, but in BSA/Triumph's case, turned into a double-edged sword when the company later tried to rationalise things by merging dealers and shifting production of certain models. In fact, this distrust between Small Heath and Meriden lasted right up until the end, and made salvaging something viable from the wreckage of the British motorcycle industry all the more difficult.

So, inevitably, there were howls of protest when it was announced in November 1964 that Tiger Cub production was being moved to Small Heath. How could a Triumph be made by BSA men? Not only that, but the Tiger Cub tooling – the dies, jigs and other essentials – were well worn by this time, which didn't improve the mood of the Small Heath men who had to work with them. Meanwhile, Meriden pointed to the fact that build quality fell and warranty problems rose once the Small Heath Cubs got out on the road. Oh, and although this Triumph was made at Small Heath, responsibility for warranty issues still rested at Meriden!

By February 1965, the Cub production line at Small Heath was up and running, though for the first few months engines, frames and everything else were shipped over from Meriden. In September 1965 the Bantam Cub was announced, with the familiar D7 frame and cycle parts plus

the Cub's 199cc four-stroke engine and four-speed gearbox. There were a few changes to accommodate it, such as an extra mount under the crankcase (the four-stroke was, of course, significantly heavier) a new exhaust pipe and an oil tank. The D7 fuel tank was well disguised by Triumph's 'mouth organ' badge and two-tone Nutley Blue and Alaskan White. It might not be a pure Triumph, but the Bantam Cub gave the same performance as its 100 per cent Meriden predecessor, and the D7's slightly larger frame gave it a bigger bike feel.

It was joined in November 1966 by the Super

Could a more subtle sharing of Bantam and Tiger Cub parts earlier on have saved the day? (Roger Fogg)

Cub, this time based on the Bantam D10 with the same frame alterations. Now there were full-width hubs (though hiding the same brakes as on the Bantam Cub) and 18in wheels, all set off by Firecracker Red paintwork. It was somehow harder to disguise the D10 as a Triumph, thanks to its distinctively shaped fuel tank, despite the Triumph 'four bar' badge. Meanwhile, the Bantam Cub continued, but with falling sales, and the last one was built in June 1967. The final Super was completed almost exactly two years later.

Some parts of the Bantam Cub story have yet to be unravelled. Researching *The Triumph Tiger Cub Bible*, Mike Estell found reference to a batch of T20 Bantam 175s, 248 of which were built between February and May 1969. These appear in the Small Heath build schedules, but not the factory despatch books, and they appear to have been based on the D10 or D14 Bushman, with T20 front forks, fuel tank and mudguards, and the Bantam 175cc engine instead of the Tiger Cub four-stroke. Or there was the batch of 46 Super Cubs, a cancelled order for Iran that ended up at Elite Motors in Tooting. These appear to have been

a mixture of parts, including D10 frame, D7 fuel tank, painted in dayglo orange.

There was also a proposal for a 'Pastoral Cub', a real back to basics machine aimed at Australian and New Zealand sheep farmers. It was to have a Cub engine, rigid frame, a platform behind the rider (for the sheepdog to sit on) and even a power take-off for sheep shearing clippers, driven from the old distributor drive shaft. A specialist bike for sheep farmers was an intriguing idea, but at the time BSA was pushing the Bushman for that market, so no more was heard of the sheepman's Cub.

Today, and indeed at the time, the Cub/ Bantams are not well thought of. They were hybrids: neither true Bantams, nor proper Triumphs, so enthusiasts of both marques tended to view them with disdain. The sad fact was that they came late, when both Bantam and Tiger Cub were near the end of their production life, outdated in many ways and struggling to sell against more sophisticated opposition. So, although Bantam Cub sales were disappointing, these were in the context of two machines past their sell-by date in any case.

. . . . this year's present was a complete mystery . . . .

6

D10: high-compression, short-lived

Big changes – Sports – Bushman – the Italian Bantam
The D10 was a Bantam milestone. It marked a
determined attempt to address two key failings
– performance and electrics – and it sought to
broaden the bike's appeal with new variants
like the Sports and Bushman. After a decade
of neglect, it looked like BSA was finally taking
the Bantam seriously again. And it needed to,
because all of its other attempts at developing
ultra-lightweights, like the 75cc Dandy, the 65cc
Beagle and various scooters, had ended in failure.
Meanwhile, the Bantam had soldiered on, losing
more and more ground to more modern small
bikes, especially from Japan.

So the D10, which replaced the D7 in July 1966,
must have seemed like really good news to BSA
dealers. Sadly, it wasn't enough – the D10 had
40 per cent more power, and proper alternator
electrics at last, but you still had to mix petrol and
oil manually, and there were signs that it had been
tuned beyond its capabilities. Sure enough, in a
1967 report, sales director, Wilf Harrison, pinpointed
BSA's desperate lack of competitive lightweights.

Things seemed a lot more cheerful when
the D10 was unveiled. Colourful, trendy adverts
showed cool, T-shirted couples zipping around
on a Bantam. "Swingalong into 1967 with a
Lightweight from BSA," read one. "HEY – you too
want a BSA Bantam!" shouted another. It was
official – at the height of the '60s, the Bantam was
a swinging thing.

And there seemed to be good cause for the
hype. A whole raft of changes saw engine power
boosted from 7.5bhp to 10bhp at 6000rpm. Higher

Bob Currie testing the new D10 – he still had a soft spot for the softer-tune Bantams. (VMCC Library)

D10 foreground, D14/4 behind, showing different tank styles. (Roger Fogg)

new crankshaft to suit the alternator, with a smaller Woodruff key (BSA had clearly learnt its lesson from the D7 crank failures) and the contact breaker points were housed behind a circular cover on the drive side. Surely here was a Bantam with zippy performance and decent, dependable lights.

As well as the mechanical changes, the range was expanded to four models. In the past, a Bantam was a Bantam, but now it reached out into niche markets previously ignored. At the bottom of the range, the Silver Bantam and Bantam Supreme looked much the same as before. Both had the 10bhp engine and alternator electrics, but made

compression (now 8.65:1), new cylinder head with greater squish band, reshaped inlet port, bigger 1in Amal carburettor with a pancake air filter, an oval-section conrod and a domed piston with two rings instead of three. An extra clutch plate was added to keep all this under control, and the air cleaner, with its perforated chrome cover (just like the big BSAs), not only looked good but helped to calm induction noise.

Bantamite prayers were finally answered with a four-speed gearbox on the Sports and Bushman. Not only that, but the old Wipac flywheel generator was finally ditched in favour of a 60-watt alternator with coil ignition. There was a

Obligatory chunk of wood supports a centre stand on its last legs. (Roger Fogg)

Testers found the D10 faster but more frenetic than its predecessor. (VMCC Library)

do with the old three-speed gearbox. The Silver remained the bargain basement version, while the Supreme took up where the old De Luxe left off, with extra chrome, polychromatic blue paintwork and a pair of stainless steel mirrors. It was all set off by white coachlining, plus white piping on the black dual seat.

All very nice, but these two more basic Bantams were still hamstrung by that three-speed box (now thankfully beefed back up to its previous spec, with two sets of splines on the mainshaft and layshaft). The chasm between second and top ratios was thrown into even sharper relief by the D10's peakier power delivery. To keep the engine buzzing, one was advised to hold first until 25mph and second until forty. The D10 would certainly do that, and in fact would rev more freely than any previous Bantam, thanks in part to the lighter mass of the alternator rotor. But high revs equalled more vibration, which was so bad that it could loosen nuts and fracture brackets – the front engine mounting also proved vulnerable. The riveted-on flywheel compression plates could come loose, with unpleasant effects; and despite the Woodruff key precautions, the new crank could also give up.

The extra oomph had come at a price of increased harshness, vibration and stress – the market might have demanded more speed, and this Bantam went some way towards meeting it, but at a cost.

Nor did the alternator electrics (still supplied by Wipac, incidentally) prove an unalloyed blessing. The days of direct lighting might have gone, but the system had suspect voltage control, and could over-charge the battery. And, as ever, you had to unbolt the seat to get at the battery, which wasn't conducive to checking whether all was well, or whether its electrolyte had boiled away.

D10 Sports

For years, youths had been chopping and tuning basic Bantams with varying success – as a first bike for 16- and 17-year-olds, how could it be otherwise? And, for the first time, BSA acknowledged that many Bantams were ridden by keen young men who hung about in cafes and wore leather.

So the new Bantam Sports was an unashamed café racer. All the cues were there. The flash Flamboyant Red paintwork, the café racer flyscreen and high-level exhaust. The seat had a racing hump, just like the 650cc BSAs, and the wheel hubs were full width (though the brakes they hid were little better than the standard ones). Folding kickstart, exposed springs on the

rear shocks, flat bars and a rectangular rear numberplate. That there was lots of chrome goes without saying, on the tank, exhaust heat shields, mudguards, separate headlight and lower forks. And to cap it all off, a great wide swage of chequered tape ran along the top of the tank.

"It took the experience gained by BSA in 18 years of the Bantam range, famous the world over for their economy and lifelong reliability. It took a team of some of the most highly skilled engineers in Britain, planning and testing until they'd achieved perfection. The result? The BSA Bantam Sports, the latest and greatest in the long Bantam tradition.

"THE BANTAM SPORTS ... A TRENDSETTER WITH A REAL KICK."

It wasn't all cosmetic either, as it came with the latest Amal Concentric carburettor, the only

A new era – Bantam Sports in all its glory. (Roger Fogg)

Not exactly pristine, but a typical autojumble sale D10. (Roger Fogg)

D10 to do so, and the four-speed gearbox was a genuine step forward. *Motorcycle Mechanics* tested a D10 Sports, with a big dynamic picture of tester Jerry Clayton cornering at speed – it wasn't exactly knee-down, but was a lot more exciting than traditional Bantam road test pictures, which were either an informative but dull static shot, or a depiction of a sensible chap riding sedately through pleasant countryside.

Jerry Clayton was in no doubt that the Bantam Sports lived up to its name. "Chasing a new sporting image," he wrote, "the Bantam has at last discarded its 'chicken's head' transfer. This is just as well because the new four-speed gearbox and increased engine performance give the bike a punch normally associated with a motorcycle twice its size!"

In fact, having four speeds to choose from seemed to make all the difference. The Sports

wasn't any faster flat-out than the three-speed D10s, as overall gearing was the same, but it certainly got there, and climbed hills, a lot more quickly. "Revs have to be kept up for hillclimbing, and this is where the four-speed gearbox comes into its own. Instead of labouring on in top ... the D10S can be dropped a cog and wound on with hardly any loss in speed." The Sports would top 62mph (not that much faster than a D5, truth be told) but could sprint to 30mph in less than six seconds, making it the quickest production Bantam yet.

Jerry Clayton also liked the handling (once the front tyre was persuaded to stop wandering around on the rim) and the "terrific grip" from the tyres. He thought the brakes not as good as their full-width hubs suggested they should be, and that the ungaitered forks allowed wet and grit into the innards. The bike had "a really handsome appearance", with "clean, sporty lines", and despite the chequered tape and high revving nature, it still sipped fuel as Bantams always had. Clayton averaged 90mpg overall and 113mpg on a more gentle tour. The Sports might look like an aspirant café racer, but it was still a Bantam at heart.

The Bushman

The Bantam Sports wasn't a new idea – the concept of a café racer had been around for a decade or more, and other manufacturers (notably Royal Enfield) had already gone down the same route. But the Bushman was different. There had been off-road Bantams before, but these had either been aimed directly at trials riders (the Competition D1 and D3) or at farmers (the D7 Pastoral). The Bushman was more adaptable than that, and aimed at being a dual-purpose bike, before trail bikes were popularised by the Japanese.

It was Peter Glover, BSA's assistant export manager, who came up with the whole idea. In the summer of 1966 he was asked to come up with something that would boost Bantam sales. "Our largest market – the USA – was distinctly lukewarm towards BSA's unsophisticated lightweight two-stroke," he later wrote in *The Classic Motorcycle*, "so my mind veered in another direction ... There must be a demand for an inexpensive workhorse with go-anywhere capability."

The next day (he had come up with the idea over a pint in his local) Peter consulted BSA's chief designer, and the Small Heath works manager, Alistair Cave. Both were keen on the idea, and

Clip-ons aren't original; chequered trim is. (Roger Fogg)

Pipe-smoking backwoodsmen would love the Bushman, or so BSA hoped. (Peter Glover)

things started to move. Guided by Peter, a commercial artist made an accurate drawing of the proposed bike in orange and white. Glover later recalled that he chose orange because no other BSA used it, and it was associated with a top selling make of agricultural machinery – Allis-Chalmers in the USA. Ted Hodgson, east coast president of BSA Incorporated, wasn't impressed, either by the idea or the colour. "He told me I was creating an agricultural motorcycle!" said Peter.

Back at Small Heath, Webster and Cave were a lot more enthusiastic, and got to work on the hardware; when Peter Glover returned from a sales trip to the USA, two prototypes had been built. Although the Bushman shared many parts with the standard Bantam, there were lots of new bits as well. The spokes and rear suspension had to be beefed-up, and ground clearance increased to a useful 10 inches. A bashplate protected the

AD SPEAK

Imagine a full-page picture showing a cool dude and pillion, all in white, on a D10. "Buy a BSA Bantam and you're part of a great tradition. Ask any of the satisfied Bantam users (and there's been a lot of them over the last 20 years). They'll agree – there's nothing to beat a Bantam for economy, smart good looks and reliability. Long life too. Every Bantam features the famous sturdy two-stroke slow-revving engine – so every Bantam will go on and on when lesser machines have fallen by the wayside. And because the Bantam's a British machine of the simplest design, spares for it are the cheapest on the market ... You're your own master on a BSA Bantam!"

D10 with later forks, rear light and all-chrome tank.
(Roger Fogg)

– about 25 per cent down – so it was flat-out at 53mph, and 40mph was a comfortable cruising speed. Fortunately, it also had the latest four-speed gearbox, which made it useable off-road, with the mainshaft and gearbox bearings uprated to suit. However, just to illustrate how fast things were running out of BSA's control, even that wasn't enough. Wilf Harrison, the company's sales director, wrote in a 1967 report that the Bushman had sales potential to Australian sheep farms, but added: "It is up against severe competition from the lightweight Japanese machines, now fitted with the standard four-speed gearbox and a transfer case to give high and low ratios." But he still thought it could do well, thanks to its torquier engine against the 100/125cc Japanese bikes. "Because of the Bushman's larger engine it should achieve success on the medium-sized stations."

crankcase, and there was a high-level exhaust, similar to that of the Bantam Sports. There were knobbly Dunlop trials tyres and higher, wider bars to made the bike more controllable on the rough stuff. The Bushman kept the D10's alternator, but used Lucas energy transfer ignition, to enable it to do without a battery. To fit the Bushman's utilitarian role, the designers also wanted a substantial rear carrier, but didn't want to lose the dual seat – after some searching, Al Cave found something suitable.

Since this was to be a serious off-road tool, and not a cosmetic trail bike, the Bushman had much lower gearing than road-going Bantams

The Bushman certainly looked good, in its Bushfire Orange and white tank, white mudguards and orange side panels. Despite what Ted Hodgson thought, most people neither knew nor cared that this was the colour of an American tractor. In any case, American sales weren't the primary aim. The Bushman did better as a utility off-road bike in East, West and Central Africa, as well as the sugar plantations of Guyana. The Kenyan artificial insemination service (for cattle) was apparently a major customer. And if the Egyptian ministry of agriculture's order for several hundred Bushmen had come through, it would have given a big boost to the Bantam and indeed the whole of BSA. Unfortunately, the Egyptians didn't have the ready cash, and wanted to pay BSA with a shipload of Red Sea shrimps!

Bushmen made the news too. Two expatriates tried to ride their Bantam up Mount Kilimanjaro. They didn't make it to the top, but the publicity was good. Nor were sales hurt in Ghana and Nigeria by the fact that in local slang, 'bush' implied a Heath Robinson contraption or something worn out. In fact, the Bushman sold quite well. BSA built 477 in that first 1967 season, and when production ended in November 1970, 3500 had left the production line. Not huge figures, but certainly better than the D7 Pastoral, which sold less than 600 in three years. All but 300 were exported, but then that was the general idea – Wilf Harrison and Peter Glover had been tasked with building up non-USA exports.

The Bushman was a genuine dual-purpose bike.
(Michael Martin)

An Italian Bantam

The Bushman and Sports were all very well, but they still weren't the fundamental changes that the Bantam really needed. Flashing indicators weren't difficult to fit, and there was a plan to do so, but it was cancelled when dealers balked at the £14 BSA wanted to add to the Bantam's retail price. "They wanted to keep it cheap," recalled Michael Martin. "There was a much slimmer profit margin on the Bantam. That's why they didn't do the four-speed gearbox for years."

Perhaps the most essential change if the bike was to be taken seriously in the late-'60s was automatic oiling. As mentioned previously, this had been considered at least twice before, and prototypes built, but they'd always been turned down on cost grounds. In the '50s, that was understandable, with petroil the standard system for commuter bikes.

But that wasn't true anymore, and the engineers tried again. Bert Hopwood recalled that they designed a face-lifted Bantam in 1966 with pumped and metered lubrication, which brought a 20 per cent power increase. "We were ready to go ahead," he wrote later, "but our new management suddenly decided to call it off." Hopwood added that he could never understand why, as the pump would have added just £3 to the cost of the machine.

An alternative to all this expensive and time-consuming R&D by BSA itself was to get someone else to make a new Bantam, and as an Italian-built Ariel, this was seriously considered. Ivor Davies had been a pillar of the advertising department at Triumph, and then BSA, before the very persuasive Harry Sturgeon came along. Sturgeon was MD of BSA in the mid-'60s, and by all accounts a breath of fresh air to the troubled corporation. "He was a man you could talk to," recalled Michael Martin. "He was dynamic and made things happen." So Mr Sturgeon was able to persuade advertising man Ivor Davies to take on the new title of 'Export Market Development Manager'.

"By 1966 the BSA Bantam was getting long in the tooth," Davies later wrote in *The Classic Motorcycle*, "and Sturgeon – an impatient man – wanted a quick replacement, just something that would suffice until BSA could produce another winner." Ivor Davies flew to Italy to see Leopoldo Tartarini, head of Italjet, and together they visited the factory of Minarelli, a well-established maker of small two-stroke engines. The plan was for Tartarini to design a frame, for Minarelli to fit an engine, and the complete bike to be sold by BSA as an interim Bantam replacement.

When the prototype arrived, it looked good,

Bantams were wind tunnel tested. (Michael Martin)

And here's a Sports getting the treatment. (Michael Martin)

a 160cc two-stroke with a claimed 10.5bhp. It still had petroil lubrication, but performance was brisk and there was a four-speed gearbox with well-spaced ratios. Minarelli had even gone to the trouble of casting Ariel badges into the side cases, as the plan was to sell this bike under Selly Oak's name. It all looked promising, but the Italian Bantam never got any further. Sadly, Harry Sturgeon died of a brain tumour in 1966, and, in the new regime that followed, the Ariel was forgotten. Ivor Davies later bought the bike and had it restored by Hughie Hancox. But in the meantime, the Bantam would have to soldier on as it was.

Why not visit Veloce on the web? – www.velocebooks.com
New book news • Special offers • Details of all books in print • Gift vouchers

62

7 D14/4: brave face, troubled family

Most powerful Bantam yet – BSA's descent

Back in 1948, having launched the new 4.5bhp D1 Bantam, BSA probably wouldn't have thought it possible that 20 years later it would still be making basically the same bike, but now with 12.6bhp.

The various plans for serious updates and new bikes had come to nothing, though work was still ongoing (see below). But in the meantime, the Bantam would have to carry on, and BSA decided to uprate it one more time. That time of course was borrowed, for even with the extra power and alternator electrics of the D10, the Bantam still looked desperately out of date, and with none of the extras that Japanese lightweights offered as standard.

Mind you, it was cheap, and at £130 16s 6d

D14/4 was the fastest Bantam yet, but for how long? (Peter Henshaw)

the new D14/4 was almost exactly half the price of BSA's own Starfire 250. Perhaps it was too cheap, for when BSA hiked the wholesale price to the Italian importer by a massive 37 per cent, it had little effect on sales.

But if BSA couldn't afford to give the Bantam indicators, or automatic oiling, bigger brakes or a five-speed gearbox, it could at least squeeze

Big downpipe, big ports, and 10:1 compression delivered 12.6bhp. (Peter Henshaw)

some more power out of the engine. That the increase was in the order of 25 per cent, with no really fundamental changes, speaks volumes for the little two-stroke. Compression ratio was upped to 10:1, thanks to thicker discs riveted to the flywheels. There were wider transfer and deeper inlet ports, with a 1⅝in exhaust pipe to suit. The combustion chamber was redesigned as well, and to strengthen the crankcases, an extra fixing screw was added.

Engineer John Dyson was working on the D14 engine and, quoted in Owen Wright's book *BSA Bantam*, remembered how the prototype was being power tested. It was a Saturday morning, but some of his colleagues were in, looked at the figures and got all excited when their calculations indicated 14bhp. John Dyson wasn't so sure, and checked again. The true figure turned out to be 12.6bhp, which was why the first 600 or so Bantams to the new spec were labelled as D13s. That was until someone got superstitious, or else realised that 'D14/4' sounded a lot snappier.

The D14/4 tag also underlined the fact that every Bantam now had the four-speed gearbox. A big paper-element air filter hid behind the right-hand side panel and all Bantams, not just the Sports, had an Amal Concentric carburettor in place of the old Monobloc. Battery maintenance

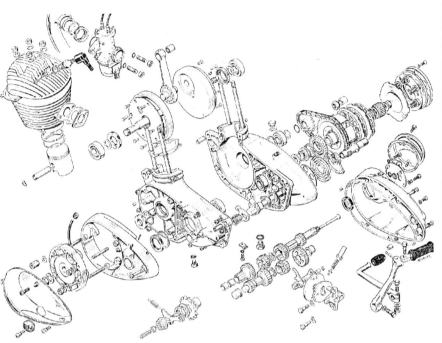

Exploded view – D14/4 was the most powerful Bantam yet. (VMCC Library)

This tatty D14 still made it up Bwlch y Groes. (Peter Henshaw)

BSA D14 175 c.c. BUSHMAN

had long been a chore for Bantam owners, who were forced to take off the seat just to get to it. Now there was an access hole in the left-hand inner panel, though unfortunately it didn't help much, being too small. Clutch adjustment was easier though, thanks to an access hole in the left-hand engine cover, protected by a rubber bung.

The entry-level Bantam Silver was dropped, and the cheapest version was now the D14/4 Supreme, very similar to the equivalent D10, and finished in black or Polychromatic Blue with white pinstriping. The Sports carried on in D14/4 form, but otherwise much the same as before. The only recognition point, apart from badging to differentiate it from the D10 Sports, was that the exhaust heatshield was in one long piece rather than two small ones. There were also different forks with thicker stanchions and rubber gaiters. The Bushman was still part of the range as well, sharing the Sports' forks and adopting its full-width hubs into the bargain.

So what did all this add up to? With nearly three times the power of the original, had the Bantam finally over-reached itself? BSA's publicity was in no doubt: "The D14/4 Bantam is the 'aristocrat' of the lightweight range", gushed the brochure, which went on to promise "well over 60mph", and fuel consumption of "at least 100mpg". Those cunning copywriters even made a benefit of petroil – "No separate oil supply to keep a check on."

Future developments

Not that BSA hadn't experimented with a posilube system. Bantam development had now moved back to Redditch, with a team headed by Michael Martin. "There were three engineers, four fitter-engineers, two designers and two testers, concentrating on two-strokes," he later recalled, "so we did a lot of work." Even so, time was at a premium, and Michael Martin would still find it a struggle to progress Bantam development. "We had to develop and build the competition engines as well, which had to be ready on a Thursday for the weekend events. It didn't help that two of the team were trials men, and tended to give priority to competition engines!"

Nevertheless, a plan was drawn up that would take the Bantam beyond the D14/4, and well into the 1970s. The short-term update on the D14 was the D18, still 174cc but with an aluminium barrel and central-plug head. It was still petroil lubed, but went well, was built into a trials frame and ridden by both Michael Martin and Mick Bowers.

The D18 was envisaged as a stop-gap, just enough of a final update to the Bantam before an all-new replacement was ready. This was to be a whole family of two-strokes from 100 to 250cc, all

They did try ... the oil pump Bantam prototype is bench tested. (Michael Martin)

Very neat, the D18 prototype. (Michael Martin)

The aluminium-barrelled D18 was to have been a stopgap until the all-new Bantam was ready. (Michael Martin)

MY FIRST BANTAM – JOHN BOLAM
"My first bike was a Bantam. I taught a friend to ride it, him sitting on the front, me on the back. We were careering down a local track, and I can't remember exactly what happened, but we ended up going through a bramble hedge. Blood everywhere, though we weren't badly hurt."

with posilube oiling. One side used a 52mm stroke, for 100, 125 and 150cc, and the other a 64mm stroke, for 175, 200 and 250cc. "They wouldn't necessarily have all been made," said Michael Martin, "but these sizes gave us the options." A 100cc single was built to test the concept, complete with Mikuni oil metering pump, housed in a mixture of Bantam and Beagle running gear, and put on test during 1969. The results were very promising: the little 100 produced 10.5bhp and averaged 74mph around the Motor Industry Research Association's test track, with a top speed of 82mph. But nothing came of the project, and John Hobday took the one-off 100 home, for his sons to use as a field bike!

The peaky Bantam
Even in its latest high-compression form, the D14/4 wasn't as fast as that 100cc prototype, but it was certainly the quickest Bantam yet. According to tests in both *Motorcycle Mechanics* and by the evergreen Bob Currie in *The Motor Cycle*, the latest Bantam topped out at 62mph, with over 40mph available in second gear and 50mph in third, the intermediate speeds at a frentic, finger-numbing 5750rpm. The power boost seemed to have brought out the best in the four-speed gearbox, with dramatically improved acceleration if you used all of those

The D14/4 Supreme looked smart in Flamboyant Blue plus pinstriping. (Peter Henshaw)

revs. From a standstill, 30mph came up in 4.1 seconds (5.9 seconds for the D10 Sports) and was nearly 6 seconds quicker than the D10 to 50mph, at 10.2 seconds. It could even climb hills at speed too, as the standard four-speed box did away with that yawning gap on the old three-speeder.

On the other hand, this wasn't the easy-going Bantam of the old days, and even Bob Currie had to admit, "it is no longer the low-speed slogger it used to be." Bob's Bantam would cruise comfortably at an indicated 60mph (a true 57mph) and he even claimed to have seen 70mph on the speedo "running before the wind". Trundle along at 30-40mph in top, and this Bantam would still deliver 100mpg, but use all the performance and those legendary fuel figures dropped off – *Motorcycle Mechanics* reported a mere 78mpg overall. Both tests praised the bike's handling, especially in town, the brakes, and the bike's honest workhorse persona. Bob even finished his test with, "who's to say that there won't be a Bantam with us another 20 years from now?" That, like BSA's brochure-speak, turned out to be a little optimistic.

A sorry background

To understand why the Bantam had been left in this state of underdevelopment, it's helpful to look at what the whole company was going through at the time. In the years after BSA's collapse, it was often accused of failing to invest. But, as author Barry Ryerson points out, the company did invest quite heavily during the 1960s – a great deal of money went into new plant, equipment and R&D, though not all of it was wisely spent.

£750,000 was spent on new plant for Small Heath in 1965 alone. Two years later, a new assembly line cost £100,000; a rolling road meant bikes didn't have to be road tested outdoors, and thus be crated up wet, salty and gritty. The new line, and an ICT 1902 computer to control production of bikes and spares made Small Heath, according to Ryerson, "the most modern assembly plant in Europe's motorcycle industry (though much manufacturing machinery remained which was worn out)."

Nor did the company squander its considerable 1960s profits in over-generous dividends to shareholders – less than half the funds available for dividend were actually handed out, and by 1968 BSA actually had cash reserves of £13 million. The trouble was, even such investment as there was, plus those cash reserves, weren't enough to completely re-equip Small Heath and simultaneously renew the entire line-up of bikes. In any case, some of this investment did go awry.

Restored D14/4 Bushman, with non-standard heat shield. (Roger Fogg)

Bantam Sports got the D14/4 treatment as well. (Roger Fogg)

Umberslade Hall, the stately home bought as an R&D centre, swallowed a massive £1.5 million each year, and BSA/Triumph employed a design staff of over 300, yet the Hall produced little useful work. Divorced from the practicalities of producing bikes, Umberslade Hall, with its peacocks strutting on the extensive lawns, was known by the cynical as 'Slumberglade'.

Michael Martin and the Redditch team were duly transferred there, with Michael given the new title of 'Chief Project Engineer – Single Cylinder', now with responsibility for the BSA/Triumph four-stroke singles as well as the Bantam and its developments, and Mike Needham as his immediate boss. "With hindsight," he said, "the

The Sports looked just the thing to take on its next-door rival, the Tiger Cub. (Roger Fogg)

main problem was that a lot of aircraft engineers were brought in. They were fine engineers, but the aircraft industry was very different to motorcycles, with long development times and small production volumes. They were used to working on a cost-plus basis, whereas we had to try and make a profit. Another thing was that every other engineer was working on a different project. It wasn't team-based, which made things difficult, and the old BSA/Triumph rivalry was still there. To be honest, I thought heads needed banging together to make it work."

Production investment sometimes went badly, too. Computerisation was a pioneering move, but bad programming led to over-production of spares, and on one occasion the faceless machine provoked a rare strike at Small Heath by miscalculating the wages. There's also the story of an expensive machine which could put a nice smooth finish on primary chaincase joints, thus reducing the chance of oil leaks. Unfortunately no one had told the man operating it that if he tossed the cases into a pile, chipping and clanging against each other, he would ruin the expensively-machined faces.

That, of course, was down to poor communication, something which Barry Ryerson puts at the heart of BSA's problems. Communication was vital to success. In the old days, warranty or production problems, and their solutions, were swiftly passed on to whoever needed to know. Now this vital flow of information, often working informally, was hamstrung by procedure. Not only that, but many of the top management and research staff had been recruited from outside the industry, ignoring homegrown talent. Sometimes this worked well (Harry Sturgeon knew very little about bikes, but he understood what needed to be done) but most of these people did not understand bikes, did not ride them or have any empathy with those who did.

That was how the 1971 twin-cylinder frame ended up too high to be ridden comfortably by anyone under six feet tall, and it was only when bikes were rolling down the production line that it was found that the engine wouldn't fit! In fact, the company seemed to lose its focus on motorcycles altogether – in 1971 the accountants Coopers & Lybrand pointed out that the board was more preoccupied with acquisitions than the process of making bikes at a profit.

Finally, BSA's increasing dependence on the booming USA market, which seemed a golden opportunity when UK motorcycle sales plummeted in the early 1960s, brought its own problems. As mentioned in the previous chapter, this was bad for the Bantam, which sold in tiny numbers across the pond, and became the Cinderella of BSA's line up as a result. And ultimately it was bad for BSA, as all its US sales depended on a short three-month selling season. If the bikes were only a few weeks late, they could miss the season altogether, and had to be either discounted heavily or shipped all the way back across the Atlantic. This happened in the months after the D14/4 was introduced. The thousands of bikes to be sold in those three months

All D14 engines had Amal Concentric carbs as well as the high compression, big-port motor. (Roger Fogg)

The AA bought Bantams, too! Jackie Lightfoot is the model. (Roger Fogg)

WORKSHOP MEMORIES – HEDLEY SLEEP
Hedley Sleep was a mechanic at Savoy Motors, a BSA dealer at St Austell in the 1960s.

"I loved them to work on, because they were so simple. I could virtually strip one down with my eyes shut. I had no problems with them at all. So if a Bantam came into the workshop, I'd jump at it, and make sure I got the job!

"There weren't many problems with them. Bottom gear could sometimes split in half and, of course, the ignition had to be kept up, but really it was a nice little bike, and I wouldn't run them down.

"But because they were so easy to work on, owners used to have a go themselves, and often they'd get halfway through a job, find they couldn't finish it and bring it in to us. A favourite thing was splitting the engine. There was a crankcase screw hidden behind the clutch, which a lot of people didn't know was there, and they'd try to prize the cases apart with a screwdriver without undoing that first! In the end they'd give up and bring it in to us. That was quite common.

"All sorts used to have them. Sixteen-year-old lads would have a Bantam as their first bike, and older men used it for getting to work on. It was really designed as a working man's bike, and often people would progress from a pushbike to an autocycle and then to a Bantam as their first motorbike. It was just right for that, as it was so cheap to run and easy to ride. They sold lots in the shop, but later on things did start to go downhill, and really it was because of the Japanese. They just did mopeds at first, but they were reliable and went well, so people bought them. When I left the dealer in 1969, things really had gone sick."

had to be built, stockpiled (and more to the point, paid for) beforehand. As we've seen, BSA did try to find alternative markets to reduce this US dependence, such as Australia for the Bushman, but ultimately it was the American market that could make or break the company, and in the end, it did the latter.

At this crucial stage in BSA's fortunes, the late Harry Sturgeon was replaced by Lionel Jofeh. Jofeh came from outside the company, and, according to Barry Ryerson, there were five candidates within BSA who could have done the MD's job (including Bert Hopwood), and each of those five men knew the motorcycle market inside out. Jofeh had no interest in bikes, and is probably now best known for an incident in the management dining room. BSA's sales director Wilf Harrison once walked in for lunch, having arrived by bike. A disdainful Jofeh remarked: "I would rather you didn't come into the Senior Management Dining Room in motorcycle attire." Which really summed up BSA's increasing distance from its core business of making bikes.

Why not visit Veloce on the web? – www.velocebooks.com
New book news • Special offers • Details of all books in print • Gift vouchers

70

B175: the final Bantam

A stronger, better Bantam – the end – rise from the ashes?

The D14/4 may have been the fastest Bantam yet, but it also brought problems of its own. Just like the D10, using all the extra performance brought vibration, harshness and sometimes fractured brackets. The engine and gearbox generally coped with the power increase, apart from the riveted-on compression discs, which could break free and wreak predictable havoc within the crankcase. "We went down to the production line, to see how they were put together," recalled Michael Martin. "It was pathetic, the way the flywheels were assembled – the riveting was unbelievably primitive, and the rivets would just fall out." There was also a spate of small-end failures,

Well restored military-spec B175, the final Bantam. (Roger Fogg)

and BSA's warranty department was certainly kept busy by the D14.

BSA might have neglected the Bantam in the early 1960s, and would never undertake the fundamental changes that might have kept it going into the '70s, but now it seemed to be making up for lost time. The D10 had lasted only a year before being replaced by the D14/4, and that in turn was dropped after a mere seven months. The bike that took over, and turned out to be the last Bantam of all, was the B175. There is some confusion as to whether this carried a 'D' or 'B'

Gaitered forks and central-plug head are B175 recognition factors. (Roger Fogg)

BSA made lots of changes to the last Bantam. (Roger Fogg)

prefix. 'D' was consistent with every other Bantam, but 'B' put it in line with the rest of BSA's range. The company used both, and for consistency we'll stick to 'B'.

Did BSA envisage that the B175 would last less than two years? It seems unlikely, as it spent a lot of money making some quite serious changes. First and most obvious, a new cylinder-head casting had the sparkplug mounted centrally, not canted backwards as on every other Bantam. It's an instant recognition point, or would be if the head wasn't a straight swap for that on the D14/4.

Those warranty problems of the D14 had evidently made their mark, as many of the internals were beefed up, and the compression ratio dropped slightly to 9.5:1. To prevent the compression discs coming loose, these were now kept in place by a rolled-in rim lock, rather than rivets, and that did the trick. The crankshaft was stiffened with bigger diameter crankpins, while the gudgeon pin, small-end bearing and piston circlips were all changed as well.

Home-brewed trail Bantam, based on a B175. (Roger Fogg)

Stronger bottom end aided longevity. (Roger Fogg)

There were now a total of seventeen screws holding the crankcases together, and the left-hand crankcase forward location dowel was made hollow. A needle-roller bearing was fitted to the clutch chainwheel and the clutch springs and contact breaker points housing were modified. Some threads were changed to Unified. It all added up to probably the strongest, most sorted Bantam engine yet, though lovers of the original D1 would probably disagree.

The cycle parts weren't neglected either, and the most obvious change here was the adoption of more substantial forks from the Triumph Sports Cub, with rubber gaiters. There were new mudguards front and rear, a new left-hand side panel, and the silencer mounting bracket was changed. The rear shocks now had exposed springs (though they still weren't adjustable) and all Bantams had the Sports-type front brake backplate.

It was quite a list, and would not have been cheap to implement – not exactly the work of a manufacturer hoping to tart-up an ageing model with some fresh paint and extra chrome. The B175 seems to have been a determined attempt to put some of the Bantam's weaknesses to rest forever. But it very nearly never happened at all. According to Michael Martin, his boss, Mike Needham, was instructed by the Board of BSA to cease all Bantam development forthwith. "I had a very young and dynamic team under me," said Michael. "People like Brian Steenson, who was a very good rider (second to Agostini in one North West 200) and a very accomplished engineer – he was a graduate of Queens University, Belfast, so he also knew a lot about two-strokes. Mike Needham

and Alan Sargent thought that all these bright young men would leave if they only had the Ariel 3 to work on."

So Bantam developments continued, though there was something of the cloak and dagger about the work. "We were fairly safe," recalled Michael Martin, "as Lionel Jofeh, the Managing Director, never came to see what we were doing, though I did have to pull a stunt once with some American dealers. They were on a visit, and I was told to keep the D18 prototype well out of sight. We managed to work it so that they just caught a glimpse of it down a corridor. Of course, they insisted on seeing it, and having a ride, and came away very impressed. Next day, I was summoned by Mike Needham and given a dressing down, but as I left he said, 'Michael, in your position I'd have done exactly the same!'"

The Sports and Bushman B175s didn't last long, being discontinued in October 1969, but the sole remaining B175 roadster carried on, offered in Polychromatic Red or Blue, and in plain black.

Despite all the changes, this final Bantam didn't look that much different to the D14/4 (the fork gaiters and central plug were the giveaways), sharing its curvy chrome panels on the side of the now familiar 'jelly mould' fuel tank. *Motor Cycle* tested a B175 early, in February 1969, as part of a BSA supplement. Some of the criticisms could have been applied to any Bantam built any time in the previous 20-odd years. The foot had to be lifted clear of the rest to make use of the long-travel gearchange. The battery was still inaccessible behind its D14-style 'access hole,' so you had to unbolt the seat to get to it. And electrics? Well, the D10's six-volt alternator system hadn't changed, complete with suspect voltage control, and the tester observed that using the brakelight caused the headlight to lose power! *Meccano* magazine, which also tested a B175, thought the bike looked old-fashioned (which was fair comment) and was still too basic, lacking even a reserve fuel tap and steering head lock.

But that was the extent of the bad news. The B175 held up another Bantam tradition in that it was cheap, at £134. And reading that *Motor Cycle* road test, a lot of the praise could have been applied to just about any other Bantam as well. The test bike was "ideal for town work ... Slim and with a low seat, it can be wriggled through traffic to the head of any hold-up with ease." And it was easy to ride – covering the Colmore Trial over icy roads would have been nerve-wracking on a heavier, more powerful bike, but "the lightness, nice balance and ease of handling of the little BSA were a boon." The reviewer liked the latest

... but instrumentation remained basic. (Peter Henshaw)

B175 forks were the best of the bunch ... (Roger Fogg)

well-damped forks, and thought the bike coped well with a ten-stone pillion, though adjustable rear shocks would have been nice.

Of course, the B175 wasn't quite as quick off the mark as the high-compression D14/4, a second or so slower to 50mph, but was actually faster flat-out, at a true 65mph. Just as important, it was

tractable, and would pull away from low revs, "with plenty of punch" as the weekly put it. The test bike had covered some serious mileage, too, which was hinted at when it was delivered with a screen and pannier frames. It had been run-in by a jaunt to the Elephant Rally. *Motor Cycle* then had it for three weeks, in the course of which another staffer rode it to Germany and back!

The end

The B175 was certainly a great improvement on the D14/4, and those road tests ended on the traditionally upbeat note, but the sad fact was that, despite the changes, the Bantam was seriously outdated and under-equipped compared to most rival lightweights, and certainly all of those hailing from Japan.

With its world about to collapse, BSA still didn't let go. Umberslade Hall had not acquired a good reputation, but after being handed responsibility for the Bantam, it wasn't idle. Michael Martin devised yet another revamp, featuring full-width hubs and upside down forks. An all-new 200cc engine was built as well, and tested in a B25 frame – it was this engine that formed the basis of Michael Martin's Mickmar engine, later built by Talon Engineering. An artist's impression of this Bantam for the 1970s envisaged, the Pinto, a road-oriented trail bike, and a proper trials machine.

In retrospect, it was surprising Umberslade had time for this, as the whole BSA range except the Bantam was renewed for 1971. All other singles and twins had the new Umberslade-designed frame, new forks, new brakes, new styling and other changes, though still based around the outdated pushrod engines. The new range was launched

Brakes weren't bad by this time. (Roger Fogg)

with a great fanfare in November 1970, first at the Royal Lancaster Hotel in London, then the Hilton. And alongside the new range, there was the B175.

It was a disaster. The trumpeted new frame turned out to be too tall for riders of average height, and as the production lines began to roll, staff at Small Heath and Meriden found that the twin-cylinder engine wouldn't fit! Production had already been delayed, and what with one thing and another, this brave new face of BSA/Triumph missed the vital US selling season of 1971 altogether, bikes only beginning to trickle onto the market in late summer.

Amid all this confusion, the Bantam was finally dropped in March '71. There was an outcry among motorcycle press and public, which was odd, considering that the latter had by this time abandoned the Bantam in favour of a Honda or Suzuki. Like that other troubled British manufacturer – BMC/Leyland – knocking BSA had become a public pastime. According to Bob Currie, the final batch of bikes were sold off by BSA dealer Cope's

Flamboyant Red B175, all complete; a good project for someone. (Roger Fogg)

The Post Office bought up some of the last Bantams, and squirreled them away. (Peter Henshaw)

The crowing logo might have gone, but this was still a Bantam. (Roger Fogg)

of Birmingham at the 1972 Midland Motorcycle Show. The Post Office also salted away a few B175s, to replace ageing telegram bikes, and the last of those didn't go into service until 1974.

Attempts at revival

Despite being dropped, it need not have been the end of the Bantam. Before Small Heath closed, a prototype called 'Budgie' was built. It was clearly a Bantam, but with Ceriani-type forks, full-width hubs and a big dual seat. By this time, Michael Martin had left BSA to work on British Seagull, the marine outboard engine manufacturer which several ex-BSA engineers would move to. He was approached by production engineer Cyril Halliwell and the Small Heath works convenor to come back

to the Midlands. With Small Heath facing closure, there was a plan to set up a workers' cooperative, as would later keep Meriden going for another eight years. They wanted Martin to come back and take this renewed Bantam back into production, using a development of the final 200cc prototype.

There were other attempts to keep the Bantam going. BSA dealer Comerfords was keen to build Bantam trials bikes. The plan was that BSA would supply standard existing parts while Comerfords would make any new parts and assemble the machines. "They were very switched on, really wanted to do it," recalled Michael Martin, "and Brian and myself went down to see them. We lobbied the management hard, but they didn't want to relinquish the manufacturing title." It wasn't just trials bikes either – there was still potential for sales to the Post Office, according to Mick Bowers.

It all fell on deaf ears. The Small Heath cooperative plan came to nothing, and to prevent anyone else taking on the Bantam, management ordered that the tooling be destroyed. Michael Martin went on to design and produce the Mickmar 250cc two-stroke engine for off-road bikes. It was based on his 200cc prototype from the Umberslade days, and owed nothing to the Bantam. This was later taken up by Talon Engineering of Yeovil, Somerset, which built 30 or 40 engines, according to Talon boss George Sartin. "In the end, we couldn't carry on," he recalled. "We had about four people developing the engine, and as there were only eight of us altogether, we couldn't afford it."

There was also talk of a deal with the Iranians. Over in Tehran, the BSA importer thought that the basic two-stroke was just the thing for Iranian conditions. The bike sold quite well there, and his proposal was to ship all the tooling over to Iran and carry on producing the Bantam there. It was an interesting idea, and with a precedent. The obsolete Hillman Hunter was built in Iran under licence long after it was dropped by Chrysler, and of course everyone knows about the Royal Enfield Bullet – sold to the Indians in the 1960s, and still being successfully built in Madras in the 21st century.

But all these plans came to nothing, and meanwhile BSA continued to struggle on. A new management team did make some progress, cutting the company's debts by half, while Bert

BSA quoted the same power as for the D14/4. (Roger Fogg)

B175 Bushman, a picture taken by Peter Glover in December 1970, on a visit to BSA's Cameroon importer. Three months later, the Bantam was dead. (Peter Glover)

Hopwood worked on his all-new modular range, from a 200cc ohc single to a 1-litre V5. The company still needed a substantial injection of cash, and the Department of Trade and Industry agreed to give it, but only if BSA/Triumph merged with its main competitor, Norton-Villiers. In the event, after BSA's share price collapsed (thanks to a speculator who didn't own any BSA shares) the promised Government support was drastically scaled down. The mighty Small Heath plant finally closed in 1975 and was demolished a couple of years later.

Fast-forward 20-odd years, and there were plans for reviving the Bantam name, but building the bike in, of all places, Germany – history was never more circular! The BSA name was now owned by the BSA-Regal group, part of whose business was importing MuZs, distant descendants of DKW. This story began when Bertie Goodman and Bill Colquhoun made a management buy-out of the remains of BSA in the late-1970s, and built a series of lighweights with bought-in engines, including the BSA Tracker trail bike and even a Yamaha-powered machine named Bushman. This new-generation Bushman was mostly exported to the Third World.

In 1986 the company moved to Blockley in Gloucestershire, and five years later merged with Andover Norton to form a new BSA Group. Another three years on, and the whole lot was taken over by Southampton engineering group Regal, and BSA-Regal was born. At the same time, MuZ bought limited rights to use the BSA name on sub-125cc bikes. Back in Southampton, BSA-Regal launched the BSA Gold SR. Built in small numbers from 1999, this Yamaha-powered 500cc single had a passing resemblence to the original Gold Star.

But more intriguing for the Bantam story was the prototype that surfaced in the press in the autumn of 1996. After the fall of the Iron Curtain, MuZ was reborn as a private concern, dropping its long-serving two-strokes in favour of the Yamaha-powered Skorpion, penned by British design house Seymour-Powell. This latest proposal was designed by Seymour-Powell too, a sharp looking bike that wore BSA badges and was intended to be the new

Bantam. Race engineers Tigcraft built the frame (though there was talk of a monocoque chassis for production) and the original intention was to fit a new British-designed 125cc engine from designer Al Melling, the man who would later draw up the Norton Nemesis V8.

When that wasn't possible, the prototype was fitted with a Honda CG125 pushrod single just to get it running, and Simon Evans rode the result for *Motorcycle Sport & Leisure* magazine in October 1996. He thought the long wheelbase and 26 degrees of rake gave the Bantam slower steering than most 125s, but that it also had "huge reserves of stability". He added that the forks could do with stiffer springs, but otherwise the bike allowed "aggressive cornering with no hint of wobble or weave".

The riding position was too far forward, but otherwise Mr Evans came away impressed: "On the evidence of one brief ride, it seems the chassis (whether steel or monocoque) could cope with any chosen engine up to 200cc. It offers poise far above its station, a true mini-motorcycle."

In the end, this fine looking prototype never got any further. MuZ found it couldn't survive independently, and went into receivership (it was later taken over by Malaysian bike maker Hong Leong). Seymour-Powell did try promoting this Bantam for the 21st century, in the hope that someone else might take it up, but no one did.

Ten years later, some of the latest generation

ARIEL PINTO

What might have been – 1971 proposal for Pinto, the Bantam replacement. (Michael Martin)

of 16- and 17-year-olds have never heard of the Bantam, or even BSA, so the likelihood of a new bike bearing the name seems less likely than ever. On the other hand, the original still thrives, giving immense pleasure to thousands of riders all over the world. And for a bike originally designed as a workhorse, that's not a bad legacy to have.

BUSHMAN SPECIAL

Trials version of the 200cc prototype – this engine eventually became the Mickmar. (Michael Martin)

9

Make it fly!

Racing – scrambling – trials – tuning

Lapping the Isle of Man TT course at 75mph doesn't sound like the sort of thing a Bantam would do. Nor does grabbing second overall in the Scottish Six Days Trial, or winning some scrambles events outright, but Bantams did all of those, and in the 1950s and '60s a huge amount of tuning lore grew around them.

Men like George Todd and John Hogan

became experts in their fields, persuading the Bantam to perform feats that no one would have thought possible in 1948. Given the right encouragement, the humble ride-to-work rooster could fly, with ultra-high 12.5:1 compression ratios and a rev ceiling of 10,000rpm or more. It was an achievement all the more remarkable because when the Bantam was launched in 1948, few people in Britain knew anything about tuning two-strokes. Things were different in Germany, where two-stroke tuning had been carried out for years. However, the Bantam tuners and competition riders would make up for that, and the Bantam Racing Club continued to thrive well into the 21st century. In Australia, too, where Bantam racing and scrambles were strong, the little bike was made to do great things.

Tuning

"TOURING! TRIALS! RACING! If you want to get ahead – get a GT100 HIGH CR CYLINDER HEAD. For sparkling acceleration plus fuel economy and long bearing life. Cast in 'Y' alloy. Ratios of 9:1, 12:1 for all Bantams and Villiers. Price 67/6d Post Free." The GT100 was designed by George Todd, whose name would become inseparable from Bantam tuning, and made by Kelston Engineering in Bristol. It was, by all accounts, a formidable piece of kit, especially for 67/6d, post free, able to stand 15 tons of pressure per square inch at a constant 300°C.

Home-brewed trials Bantams were often real hybrids.
(Roger Fogg)

John Bass was an active Bantam racer in the 1960s and early
'70s. (Bantam Racing Club)

Home-built sprinter, evidently based on an ex-GPO bike!
(Roger Fogg)

Prolific motorcycling author,
Roy Bacon, also raced a Bantam.
(Bantam Racing Club)

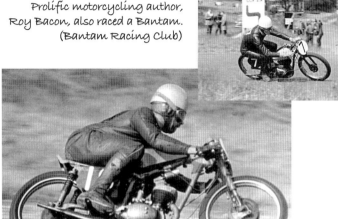

George Todd's introduction to making Bantams go fast was via his friend 'Bunny' Armstrong, who entered his Bantam in a Silverstone race in 1949, and was probably the first person to ever race one of the little birds. Todd became interested and was hooked. He amassed his knowledge the hard way, by long hours of experimentation, and raced his own Bantam as well as tuning them for other people. In 1956 he wrote the results of this experience in a booklet titled *Boost your Bantam*. A shorter version was published in *Motorcycling* that same year and, as the ultimate accolade, BSA reprinted the article and issued it to aspirant Bantam tuners via its service department. Not that BSA didn't have its own in-house two-stroke tuning experts – Brian Stonebridge and Hermann Meier had coaxed 100bhp/litre out of the Bantam in scrambles trim.

The Hogan brothers were another well-known name in Bantam tuning and racing circles. They set up shop in Pinner Green, Middlesex, and from 1953 offered their own 'high torque' cylinder head. This offered a 9:1 compression, had around three times the cooling area of the standard head and came with a central plug. The fitting kit included a timing strip and a suitable sparkplug. The Hogan head proved popular for road Bantams as well as the racing bikes, though Roy Bacon later wrote that those seeking to raise the compression ratio further were rewarded with it cracking along the centre line. However, it was Todd who became Britain's leading Bantam tuning guru, and his article in *Motorcycling* reads virtually like a Haynes manual, taking the reader through

every step of the process and dividing the whole operation into three: simple methods, intermediate and advanced, with the simple jobs possible without recourse to a well-equipped workshop. Not everyone wanted to race their Bantam, and by using the simpler stages only, it was possible just to add a bit of pep for the road. Raising the compression ratio a little, retarding the ignition and re-jetting the carb would make a useful difference. More extensive work, including re-gearing, could see a 125cc Bantam hit a genuine 65-70mph yet still be tractable enough for road use. Of course, the bike's legendary economy would suffer if one used all of that performance, with 70-80mpg quoted for 'fast touring'.

The first step, before doing any tuning at all, was to follow the advice of wise tuners everywhere – make sure the rest of the bike is in good condition. There was no point in spending time and effort extracting a 10 per cent power increase, only for the result to be swallowed by binding brakes, under-inflated tyres or a slack, dry chain. The engine too had to be in tip-top condition to make it worthwhile tuning. Just ensuring that everything was just as it should be could make a difference.

On an early Bantam (remember the advice was published in 1956) the Oilite bronze bush in the magneto stator plate had to be in perfect condition, as wear here put extra stress on the main bearings, and subsequent failure, especially when using higher compression ratios. Bore wear should not be more than 0.005in, and if a rebore was necessary, Todd advised the barrel be honed

Neat conversion, but the changes aren't as extensive as in Bantam racing. (Roger Fogg)

to 0.001in oversize, which allowed the fitting of a chrome piston ring in the top groove. As for big-end wear, he added that he had ridden a Bantam two-up for 1500 miles with 0.012in, underlining the little BSA's ability to keep going when seriously ill. Nevertheless, the official limit was 0.003in, or for the majority owners who didn't own a dial gauge, if up and down movement was just perceptible, there was about 0.015in of play and the big-end was worn out. There had to be no perceptible play at the small-end. Finally, the piston, barrel and exhaust would be treated to a good decoke and clean. George Todd recommended fitting a post-1954 exhaust, with its removable baffles.

Increasing the compression ratio on a D1 Bantam was relatively easy. Removing the raised shoulder on the cylinder head raised compression from the standard 6.5:1 to 8.5:1. An even quicker (though more expensive) option was to bolt on a GT100 or Hogan head. Either way, to suit the higher compression the timing had to be retarded, which meant lengthening the stator plate's cutaways by filing. Rejetting the carb was the next step (George suggested starting with a 110 and reducing the jet size until the plug was a nice dark brown after a burst of full throttle). Finally, the plug itself would have to be a cooler running grade.

The intermediate stage dealt more with improving the motor's breathing, with work on the ports and piston skirts, with either a small power drill, or 'riffler files and elbow grease.' Enlarging the inlet, exhaust and transfer ports by exact amounts gave longer opening times and allowed the engine to rev higher – the standard transfer period worked up to about 6000rpm. Each port had to be smooth and clean. To avoid the piston skirt getting in the way of gas flow, this had to be trimmed as well, with a chamfered (not radiused) edge. George recommended replacing the standard air cleaner with a bellmouth intake tube. With that lot, and a 110 main jet, the Bantam would fly, though he thought it should still manage 90mpg at 50mph.

For the really serious, perhaps those aiming to take their Bantam racing, Mr Todd recommended a bigger still inlet port (though not more than 7/8in diameter, if you wanted to keep some low-down

power) and an Amal 275 carburettor, with a Tufnol spacer to protect it from the heat. Steps and corners were smoothed off between crankcase and transfer ports, and fitting Dural padding plates inside the crankcase could increase compression still further. A much cheaper dodge (though possibly less durable, and it certainly wasn't mentioned by Mr Todd) was to glue shaped pieces of balsa wood into the con-rod cutaways, with Araldite adhesive! The extra heat and high revs would show up deficiencies in the main bearing oil delivery, and the oil duct could be opened out with a drill. The ultimate answer was to fit a Pilgrim oil pump, which Todd said had been used on his racing Bantam for five years, with no main bearing failures. Finally, experimenting with gear ratios, by juggling both internal ratios and gearbox sprocket, would optimise the Bantam's performance for whatever was required.

These advanced tuning techniques needed a high degree of competence (not to mention welding plant and a lathe) but they didn't cost the earth, and whichever tuning method was used, the little two-stroke would respond. It just underlined how fundamentally right it had been in the first place.

Trials & scrambles
It doesn't take long for trials clubmen to spot potential, and the first Bantam had it in spades.

Light weight and manoeuvrability made the Bantam easy to ride off-road. (Roger Fogg)

Lightweight, simple and affordable, with that tractable engine, it was obvious to onlookers that here was an ideal trials bike just waiting to be let out. Many clubmen bought Bantams straight away, and built their own lightly modified trials machines. Others pestered BSA to build an official one, and they must have been persuasive, as the D1 Competition was launched just a year after the road bike made its debut.

Rather than just make a few modifications and hope for the best, BSA actually entered the Competition prototype in several events. As for test riders, the company had plenty of top-notch trials riders on the books, such as Fred Rist and John Nicholson, but they were all busy on the big four-strokes. But there was plenty of in-house talent as well, and BSA MD Bert Perrigo (who had been a highly successful trials rider himself) picked out George Pickering from the factory road test staff.

Pickering had done a little competition riding before and after World War II, and had little time to practice on the Bantam, but immediately took to it. In fact, he won the 125cc Class Cup in the Colmore Trial, the lightweight's very first event. He went on to win six 125cc cups during 1949/50, and it was clear that Pickering was a gifted trials rider, and that the Bantam was ideal for the purpose.

Other riders soon caught on, and in the next three years the Bantam won as many 125cc cups in national trials as any other make. One such rider was George Fisher, who went on to become a Francis Barnett works rider, but started out on a Bantam. Success was more elusive in the International Six Days Trial, and in 1950, despite seven private Bantams and two factory bikes entered, none of them did well. One bike did manage a gold medal the following year, when the ISDT was held in Italy, and George Pickering was heading for one when he hit a rock in 1954, having to settle for silver.

Meanwhile, the little Bantam was proving its worth in scrambles as well. As early as 1950, Bill Nicholson won the 125cc class in the Cotswold Scramble. More Bantam wins in national scrambles events followed, especially prized by BSA, as the marque's strength in scrambles meant that a win in the 125cc class could complete a grand-slam, with wins across the board. The Experts Grand National of 1956 was a particularly glorious event for the Bantam – Brian Stonebridge and John Draper had a disastrous start, and were last away, but

Bantams quickly became favourites for trials. (Roger Fogg)

fought their way back through the entire field and finished 1-2.

When the 148cc D3 Competition came along, it was business as usual, and in an echo of that first win by George Pickering, John Draper won first time out on the D3 Comp prototype. He went on to win the 175 Class Cup in the Scottish Six Days, sixth overall and tying with Sammy Miller (Ariel) on points. But by the late 1950s, the Bantam enjoyed less success in national events, increasingly hampered by its three-speed gearbox. Of course, it remained a favourite for clubmen – a lightweight, affordable and tuneable trials bike that was ideal for a spot of weekend competition. Long after BSA dropped its own Competition model, riders were modifying road Bantams for trials, and they still do.

However, in the mid-1960s the bike had a final flash of glory at national level, thanks to the D10. With a four-speed gearbox, more power and stronger forks, this had the ingredients to be more competitive, and BSA competitions manager Brian Martin thought it had the potential to challenge the 250 Greeves and Bultaco, which were then dominating the class. A prototype D10 trials was ready by December 1966 (its engine prepared by Brian's brother Michael, who worked at Redditch) and Brian rode it in a local trial. Although no longer an active trials rider, he finished second to Ken Sedgley on a 250 Bultaco.

Class wins in national trials followed in the next few months, and Dave Rowland topped them all by managing second overall in the 1967 Scottish Six Days. It was a tremendous achievement, underlined by the fact that the only man who beat him was Sammy Miller on a Bultaco. In the elation following this, there was hope of a run of replica D10 trials bikes at the factory, but BSA's wobbly financial position in 1967 put an end to it. A brand new trials BSA was on the drawing board in 1969, but once again, the company's finances prevented it going any further.

Although the Bantam's days of national glory were over, it remained a stalwart of local trials for the next 30 years. So much so, that in 2001 Alan Wright began offering a brand new trials frame to accept the Bantam engine. It was a copy of the original works frame, though improved and strengthened here and there – so in the end, a very few riders did get the chance to buy a factory replica.

Racing

Maybe the success of the Bantam in trials isn't so hard to understand – lightweight and manoeuvrable with a nice, tractable engine.

Swift work at a service stop for this swingarm trials Bantam. (Roger Fogg)

Trials and scrambles were seen as part of the Bantam's development process. (Michael Martin)

Frame, engine, wheels, suspension – all you needed.
(Roger Fogg)

Brian Steenson was an accomplished off-road rider as well as development engineer. (Michael Martin)

Michael Martin, too, was a keen trials rider. (Michael Martin)

RACING DOWN UNDER

The Australians had a soft spot for the Bantam, and this showed up as much on the race track as on sheep farms. As early as 1950, a young man named Albert Flood, who by day assembled new BSAs for a Melbourne dealer, won a whole string of 125cc races on his Bantam, including two championships and five Ultra Lightweight TTs.

Flood's Bantam ran on alcohol, with a 15:1 compression (he had tried 17:1) formed by reshaping the combustion chamber. At the same time, he moved the plug to the central position. He spent a lot of time cleaning and polishing the ports, though the Bantam's bottom end was left standard. A big (1$\frac{3}{16}$in) Amal TT carburettor and a 14in long megaphone were other modifications. The result, according to IoM TT rider Harry Hinton, was the fastest 125 he had seen racing during 1950.

But Australia's best known Bantam racer was Eric Walsh. Eric didn't do the riding himself, having sustained a serious injury pre-war, but in the same year that Albert Flood was racing his Bantam, developed his own. It would go on to win just about every race it was entered – on both tarmac and dirt – in the next six years. Bantams didn't just grab class wins either. Maurie Quincy won the Australian TT on the Walsh Bantam in 1952 and '54, while in '52 Ken Rumble came home first in the Victoria 500cc scramble event, beating a whole host of 500cc singles and twins in the process. Moto Guzzi works riders Bill Lomas and Dickie Dale tried out an alcohol-fuelled Walsh Bantam. They both broached 100mph, and the bike was thought to be the fastest 125 in the world at the time.

Eric Walsh topped all this off by going for the Australian 125cc speed record, building a streamlined, cigar-shaped machine with full enclosure. It reached 115mph, and would have gone faster, but ignition problems prevented it.

The Bantam might have been designed, developed and intended as a stolid, reliable ride-to-work bike, but there was another side to its characters, as generations of club racers and trials riders will testify.

Fred Launchbury was one of the best known Bantam racers – he lapped the Island at over 70mph. (Bantam Racing Club)

Roy Bacon lapping Alan Brown – Bantam racing was close. (Bantam Racing Club)

Bantam racers used their ingenuity – impressive-looking front brake on this bike at Snetterton. (Bantam Racing Club)

Superb shot of a Bantam racer getting down to it at Thruxton. (Bantam Racing Club)

But racing? It's harder to envisage this humble ride-to-work bike taking the chequered flag at Silverstone. And yet, the Bantam's tuneability and (as with the trials crowd) affordability, made it an ideal clubman's racer. As well as the many weekend racers, there were others who went on to bigger things after starting their racing career on a Bantam, among them Barry Sheene and Formula One driver Damon Hill. It wasn't just in Britain either – Australia had a strong racing Bantam scene, and even the Americans were in on the act. Ray Weiman won the 125cc class in the Catalina Grand National, a punishing mountain road race, in 1952 – and he wasn't the only one. Bantams took four of the top five places.

Bunny Armstrong might have been first to race a Bantam, but by 1950 it was so popular that 125cc races were being organised. Just as in trials, running your own Bantam was one of the cheapest ways to go racing at weekends, and though there was never a factory racing Bantam, this was made up for by countless keen privateers. The racing was hard and fast, and a good training ground for novice riders. There were so many of them that the Bantam Racing Club was formed in 1960, initially based around the Wimbledon MCC, with Bunny Armstrong a prominent member.

The BRC became one of the pillars of British club racing, keeping the rules as simple as possible. This had two effects: simple rules encouraged lots of people to have a go, but they gave scope for the more inventive to use their imagination. Within the early rules of using the original frame and crankcases, 125cc and three speeds, there was a lot of leeway. One favourite dodge to boost braking power was to weld two front hubs back to back. The same principle was later extended to the gearbox – using two clusters gave five speeds!

As the years went by, the technology

TRIALS – GEOFF NUTT

"A friend of mine was using his wife's Bantam in trials, but on the day he couldn't ride and asked me. I was pleasantly surprised by the bike, and even more so that by the first break I found that I was leading! Of course, later in the day all the younger chaps on big Triumphs came past me, but it said a lot for the Bantam. It was very easy to ride, and well suited to trials."

Race transport, circa 1960. (Bantam Racing Club)

developed. In the 1960s, most racing Bantams still used points ignition with standard flywheels, big-ends and con-rods, but some racers were making more radical experiments. Fred Launchbury developed a type of rotary inlet valve, which included an oil pump that fed the valve to avoid seizure. It's thought that the device was chain driven, but it was later dropped by Fred, for unknown reasons.

In any case, power increased through the 1970s, and as the bottom-end cried enough, Alpha con-rods and big-ends became popular, along with smaller, lighter flywheels. Points ignition was still common, though a lot of the top-flight racers used early self-generating systems (eg Motoplat) or an electronic car system adapted to suit – Lumenition was one early electronic ignition. Water-cooling was increasingly used, adapting the standard cylinder barrel. Modern forks were fitted to racing Bantams, and as power broached the 20bhp barrier, even the Alpha rods came under serious stress. Then someone discovered that reliable, high-revving Japanese internals could be squeezed inside the original crankcases.

It was an open question as to whether these water-cooled short-stroke engines had that much in common with a Bantam, but they were still within the letter of the rules. After many years of development, the racing Bantam could be highly competitive. From 1985, the BRC ran Open class events, in which Bantams could be racing against TZ125 Yamahas, but in the '87 season Bantam rider Mike Powell beat them all. His highly-modified bike was typical of the more serious breed, with a water-cooled jacket, RD250 flywheels, TZ250 big-end and RM125 Suzuki piston. And despite driving through a three-speed gearbox, it could crack 106mph at 12,000rpm.

The 1990s saw still more power, with some racers claiming as much as 24bhp, and there was more to come in 21st century. By 2007, some racers used all-aluminium barrels (Alan Brown's was typical) with modern plated bores. Some of the early Bantam race bikes could top 100mph, but often took an entire straight to get there – the modern, tricked-up Bantams could crack the ton in a few hundred yards! Alan predicted that power would reach close to 30bhp by 2010, and the Bantam Formula saw a slowly increasing number of new and returnee racers choose the bike as a cheap route to circuit experience. One increasing problem was a lack of gearboxes, especially as the old three-speed close-ratio clusters were now under severe stress from double the power they were originally designed for. It was hoped that further development would solve this though. As Bantam racer Alan Brown wrote in 2007, "They are really 'works racers from the shed' in every sense!"

Bantams weren't restricted to short circuits either, and the Bantam Racing Club actually won

And the Bantams haven't stopped ... Alan Brown and friends at Lydden. (Bantam Racing Club)

BANTAM RACING CLUB
125 formula regulations
1. CAPACITY All machines will be 125cc. Oversize pistons to +2mm allowed on any engine, and 58mm long-stroke engines (normally 52mm bore) are allowed to use up to and including 55mm pistons, allowing the use of modern available equipment.
2. ENGINE Modifications to engine or gearbox are allowed, provided that conditions a) to e) below are met:
a) Bantam crankcases must be used
b) Disc valve induction is prohibited
c) Pressurised fuel injection is prohibited
d) Only BSA close-ratio gears and BSA normal-ratio gears or exact copies (eg AA Snell) to be used. Maximum number of gears: Three.
e) Only standard cylinder barrel to be used but may be modified internally. (Alloy Todd and BTW copies deemed to be standard but to remain air-cooled, not liquid-cooled).
3. FRAME Must retain Bantam main loop, but may be modified.
4. WHEELS Must retain wire-spoked wheels.
5. BRAKES Front brake – No restrictions except Wavy or Carbon Fibre discs not permitted.
Rear brake – Bantam rear hub to be retained but may be modified.
6. FORKS No modern 'upside-down' forks may be used, although original Bantam upside-down forks are permitted.
7. TANK Must be mounted in normal position on machine.
8. FUEL Only Petrol or Avgas 100LL mixture to be used.
9. ACU standing regulations for road racing machines apply (where applicable).

175 formula regulations
1. CAPACITY All machines will be of 190cc capacity maximum.
2. ENGINE Modifications to engine and gearbox are allowed, provided that conditions a) to l) below are met:
a) Bantam crankcases must be used, and remain externally unchanged, except for increasing stud centres to 60mm, on 52 or 55mm versions.
b) Stroke to remain standard (58mm).
c) Disc valve and reed valve induction is prohibited.
d) Pressurised fuel injection is prohibited.
e) Only BSA close-ratio and BSA normal-ratio gears or exact copies (eg AA Snell) to be used. Maximum number of gears: Three if close-ratio, and four if normal road ratios.
f) Only standard cylinder barrel to be used, but may be modified internally. (Alloy Todd and BTW copies deemed to be standard but to remain externally unchanged).
g) Cylinder stud centres not to exceed 60mm.
h) Water-cooling prohibited.
i) Ignition to be fixed timing (ie not advancing or retarding type), however Ducati Energer and PVL straight line (maximum 4 degree retard) are allowed.
j) Exhaust power valves are allowed.
3. FRAME Must retain Bantam main loop, but may be modified.
4. WHEELS Must retain wire-spoke wheels.
5. BRAKES Front brake – No restrictions except Wavy or Carbon Fibre discs not permitted.
Rear brake – Bantam rear hub to be retained but may be modified.
6. FORKS No modern 'upside-down' forks may be used, although original Bantam upside-down forks are permitted.
7. TANK Must be mounted in normal position on machine.
8. FUEL Only Petrol or Avgas 100LL mixture to be used.
9. CARBURETTOR Size: 38mm maximum, circular bore only.
10. ACU standing regulations for road racing machines apply (where applicable).
11. Any rider winning the Bantam Championship on a 175cc machine must progress to 125 thereafter.

the Team Award in the 1989 Production TT! That was no misprint, but naturally many BRC members raced other bikes as well, and Bantams really did race on the Island. Two finished the Ultra Lightweight TT in 1951, the faster being L Caldecutt, in ninth at 56.30mph, while the following year, H Williams managed seventh. The fastest Bantam at the TT was that ridden by Fred Launchbury in 1967. The bike he rode was actually an ex-GPO machine, but had been worked on by the legendary George Todd, and Fred averaged 73.9mph. That he

finished 20th was just a reflection on how far the Japanese and Continental 125s had come in the meantime.

As for the Bantam Racing Club, that collapsed in the 1990s, but a number of hardy souls battled on, and the ashes of the BRC came to rest with the VMCC Racing Section, later known as the British Historic Racing Club. The Bantam Racing Club still thrives, on an informal basis, as does Formula Bantam racing.

10 Adventure by Bantam

Epic trips – pass bagging – I'm Bantam, Fly Me – the Wall of Death

<u>FLORIDA TO GEORGIA</u> – <u>ARDEN JENSEN</u>

The summer between eleventh and twelfth grade had been our golden time. Mike and Dudley had Vespas, Hugo had a Harley Sprint, and Robert was the king of the group by virtue of his Norton Electra. I had my trusty 1962 BSA Bantam. It was the summer of 1963 in Miami, Florida.

Every day we would get up as late as we wanted, scavenge a few bucks by mowing a lawn or cashing in soda bottles or begging from a parent or doing whatever we could that did not involve too much time and effort. Gas was 25 cents per gallon. And at the gas station I usually drained the drops of oil that remained in the cast-off oil cans into the measuring cup on the bottom of my gas cap. The Bantam was not very picky about what went into the tank, and every gallon of gas would get me about three hours of cruising time.

We would pool our money and buy smokes and, if we could find a buyer, quart bottles of cheap beer. We would sneak off to the woods, drink the beer, smoke the cigarettes, and then ride. Sometimes we could find wild girls who would sneak out with us. What a life! Ah, to be sixteen again in a more innocent world.

At the end of that summer, the gang had to

Climb every mountain? Or in this case, nearly to the top of Mt Kilimanjaro, by Bantam. (Peter Glover)

break up. Dudley's family was moving to Chicago. If he wanted to keep his Vespa, he would have to ride it the 1000 miles or so to Chicago. Since I had friends in northern Georgia, about 500 miles away, I decided to go with him. My dad, who was always open to my adventures, gave me a few dollars and wished me well.

We did not ride fast, between 40 and 45mph (about maximum cruising speed on both the Bantam and the Vespa), but we rode long. By the first night we had made 300 or so miles and slept, or at least tried to sleep, under the trees beside the road. Early the next morning we continued northward. In those days before the Interstate System, the highways had personalities. No one in a car can understand a road the way a motorcyclist can. Each groove, each bump, and each hole is waiting to turn aside or swallow a wheel, so the rider has to know what is in front of him. The roads ran through swamps, up and down hills (some of which required second gear), and through farmland, tiny villages without even a stop light, and some fair-sized small towns.

South Georgia is hot in late August, well over 100°F, which I believe is around 40°C. It was like riding through a warm bath. Late in the afternoon we entered the North Georgia mountains, which meant a laborious 30mph or so in second gear uphill and a blood-chilling 60-plus down the other side with the clutch held in. Yes, dear reader, Bantam brakes do fade. I knew two pretty girls, one in Dooley, north of Blairsville, Georgia, the other in Suches, to the south. Jennifer, who lived in Dooley, close to where we were staying, ended up liking Dudley. Mary Jo, my best hope, was thirty miles away through the mountains.

She invited us to an outdoor cook-out at a park one evening. We went back to bathe, change, and prepare ourselves for seeing those pretty Georgia girls. Mary Jo, by the way, had flawless white skin, dark brown hair, and deep blue eyes. Why she ever wanted anything to do with a pimpled, ugly adolescent boy is beyond me. The Bantam ran out of gas on the way up the mountain, and by the time we finally got to the cook-out, it was over. We had missed our chance at becoming the main men at the social event of the season.

Flashbulb Bantam

The only time the Bantam itself did me wrong on this trip was one dark night when I was going up a steep hill. The engine was bogging down in third, so I quickly let off the gas, pulled in the clutch, mashed down with my right foot, let out the clutch and grabbed a handful of throttle at the same time. The entire world lit up for an instant.

I had missed the gear and the mighty Wipac AC generator pumped out enough juice to turn the headlamp into a flashbulb. Luckily, in the great wisdom of Birmingham Small Arms, another beam had been provided. I reasoned that tail lights are not that important because there is a reflector in the lens.

By then, Dudley's Vespa had eroded its sparkplug to the point that he had to start the scooter by getting a good downhill roll and letting the clutch out in first gear. We did not have enough sense at the time to know what was wrong. We parted ways — he did make it to Chicago, and I set out for Miami.

One part of my toolkit was a roll of straightened coat hangers and a pair of pliers — one never knows when some exotic bolt and/or nut will fall off and require a quick repair. On the way back home, I pulled into a North Florida gas station and heard a man complaining about the strap that held his gas tank on his Ford station wagon. I crawled under his car and put the strap back into place with one of my coat hangers. He gave me a buck — enough to buy several hundred miles' worth of gas. I finished my journey by riding all night, adjusting from high to low beam by twisting the headlight unit up or down. Actually, as I recall, the light was dim to the point of not making much difference anyway.

All of us have our adventures as we grow up. The Bantam and I had ours. The thousand-mile round trip was just one of those escapades. I still have the Bantam. I had traded it in on a Zundapp Super Saber, perhaps the worst motorcycle I ever owned. Later, I found the remains of my Bantam in a motorcycle junkyard. Some other kid almost totally destroyed what had been my pride and joy.

I retrieved what was left and carried the parts around with me for over thirty years. Just this past summer I decided to resurrect the Bantam into the kind of hot rod motorcycle I dreamed of when I was sixteen. I pieced together a D5 engine, made an expansion chamber, fitted folding footpegs (remember dragging the pegs hard enough to pick up the wheels and put the bike on the ground?), and rounded up parts to make the Bantam look sporty and go a bit faster. Who knows what will make golden memories? I still smile as I remember the pretty girls in Georgia, the half-warm beer we drank while hiding in the woods, and the Bantam.

THE APPLECROSS CLIMB – BRIAN MOORE

The Bantam (B175) was taken to the West Coast of Scotland during the dubious 'summer' of 2000, when it rained solid for days. I had rebuilt the bike from two tea-chests one winter.

At the summit.
(Brian Moore)

Brian Moore's B175 halts on Rannoch Moor. (Brian Moore)

No learners, no caravans ... but small BSAs are fine.
(Brian Moore)

The first day out from Benderloch, near Oban, we headed for Fort William and then through Glen Coe, across Rannoch Moor and back to Benderloch. Next day we rode across the Atlantic Bridge to the Isle of Seil, where there used to be a whole community making their living in the slate quarries.

I wanted to visit Ardnamurchan lighthouse, the most westerly point of the British Isles, which included crossing onto the Peninsula on the Corran ferry – the Corran Narrows can be very turbulent, the water looking as if it is boiling at certain tides. After leaving the ferry, the road just got narrower and narrower, but the views were brilliant.

From Plocton, I planned a run up to Achnasheen, and away we went in the pouring rain, the Bantam and I. But when I saw the Applecross road on the left, one look at the warning sign was enough – it simply had to be conquered by Bantam. And it was! The weather at the top was thick sea fog, coming in on strong westerly winds. So, a quick cup of coffee and a fast descent of Applecross to the Torridon road, then north to Kinlochewe. I later found out that the sea fog was all along the coast road from

the Atlantic coast town of Applecross, so there wouldn't have been spectacular views that way anyway.

The Bantam just wanted to carry on, but with the sea fog coming in, a run back down the Torridon road seemed like a good idea. The following day I made the long haul up to Gairloch to see some old friends before heading back to Benderloch. The Bantam never faltered at any stage of the journey, and is still going strong.

ACROSS THE SAHARA BY D7 – JULIAN PREECE

Julian Preece's plan was to ride from Northampton to India on his 1966 D7 Bantam. His preparations consisted of an engine rebuild, packing a few spares and rubber-mounting a one-gallon petrol can to each rear shock, but he had no Carnet de Passage to aid border crossings, and the bike's engine number differed from that on the documentation. "Most border guards looked at the bike, then at each other, had a good laugh and waved me on," he wrote later in *Classic Bike*.

He got as far as Turkey, where the Iranian embassy told him he'd have to wait two months for a visa to get into Iran, so he decided to head for Africa instead. Through Syria and Jordan, then a boat to Suez before riding to Cairo and waiting for a Sudanese visa.

Riding down through Egypt, the Bantam wasn't running well, and the kickstart sheared off, but a backstreet mechanic fitted a new one about two feet long. He was now averaging 32mph ('the speed at which the bike felt most comfortable') and was getting 90mpg.

Julian crossed the Aswan Dam, entered Sudan and was shocked at the state of the road, then consisting of a wide stretch of sand, with tyre tracks heading in all directions. He took to a railway track on the way to Khartoum, bouncing over the sleepers. The forks had

An Alpine Pass? No, but Bantams did those, too. (Brian Moore)

long since lost all their oil and often bottomed out on their weak springs, but stayed together. If the Bantam got stuck in sand, Julian jumped off and ran alongside.

He travelled to Bangui in the Central African Republic, where the French Father at a Catholic Mission turned out to have two D14 Bantams. Neither was running, but the priest did allow Julian to cannibalise them for spares.

Eventually, it was time to head northwards, and home. "It was now April and beginning to get hot. I was not looking forward to the Sahara." Preparations included buying three cans of sardines, but unfortunately $150 was stolen in Cameroon. He had to declare $220 at the Algerian border to be allowed into the country, which left Julian and the Bantam with $30 to cover the 2500 miles in between.

Meanwhile the Bantam was in poor shape, with piston ring gaps nearly half an inch across. Violent crosswinds carried sand, which got inside the carburettor, seizing the throttle slide, despite Julian's precaution of covering the air filter with an oil-soaked sock. Tahoua to Agadez (260 miles) took three days. With temperatures reaching 40°C, rider and bike "began to wilt" but he did meet a Citroën 2CV driver going north. They travelled together "over 800 miles of corrugated rocks, bulldust and soft sand".

After seven days, they had crossed the Sahara, but both Bantam and rider were exhausted. Julian went down with a fever for three days, and as for the Bantam: "The front mudguard stays had sheared and a few spokes had broken, the mechanical noise had become louder than the exhaust as the big-ends and mains had worn. Both sprockets were almost round and the chain was like elastic; the carburettor was temperamental and began flooding at random. Basically the bike was a wreck, but it still moved forward."

With some money sent by his father, Julian was able to ride all the way home through France, though he was stopped by the police for doing 20mph on the hard shoulder of the M20. Finally back home, the Bantam went off to Charlie's Motorcycles in Bristol for a rebuild, while Julian went down with malaria, though he soon recovered.

(Julian's account of his epic trip first appeared in *Classic Bike*, January 1987.)

The airborne Bantam – Maurice Smith

In 1951 Maurice Smith, then editor of *Flight* magazine, found a novel way of ensuring that he and his wife had transport after they touched down in southern France – he squeezed her

rigid-frame D1 Bantam onto the back seats of a twin-engined Miles Gemini aircraft.

Of course, it had to be dismantled first. They removed the Bantam's front forks (with wheel in place), the rear wheel, mudguards and handlebars (with all controls except the brakes left connected). With those parts strapped to the tank, two people could manhandle the bike carefully over the Gemini's thin, ply-covered wing, and manoeuvre it into the cockpit. The whole process took 30 minutes.

Bantam secured, they took off from Woking, landing to refuel at Le Touquet where customs needed a carnet for the bike as well as the plane. That was OK, but Maurice found that 10 days insurance for the Bantam cost as much as a whole year at home! They flew on to Tours and Carcassonne, the walled medieval town on the French side of the Pyrenees, where the Bantam was extracted from its back seat, bolted back together and ridden into the old fortified city.

It attracted lots of interest, because Bantams were rare that far south. The French admired the modern telescopic forks and the foot change, but thought the tyres were a bit small. With the Bantam at their disposal, Mr and Mrs Smith were able to make forays into the countryside. They found they could cover 40-50 miles in a morning without getting tired, and the Bantam's small panniers could carry lunch. They buzzed up to the Black Mountain area one day, and over to Valras-sur-mer on the Mediterranean coast on another. The Bantam tackled mountain tracks as well as tarmac, and took the Smiths through tiny villages. They found a traditional French inn at the town of Revel, where "several tasty and wholesome courses" with wine came to 10 shillings for the two of them.

At the end of the holiday, they dismantled the Bantam again, reloaded it and took off, flying back to England via Toulouse. Visibility worsened near Gatwick, so they followed the railway through Reigate and along to Dorking and Guildford, thence back to land at Woking. "By 8.30pm, the Bantam was back in its home shed."

Lands End-John O'Groats (twice) – Ken Ascott

Not many people have ridden Lands End to John O'Groats on a Bantam, let alone twice (once each way). Make that a 1956 plunger D1, and you've summed up Ken Ascott's achievement.

Ken never set out to own a Bantam. He had a Honda 400/4, which he was happy with, but found it needed so little maintenance that he had spare time on his hands! Then his brother offered him his D1 to get running, so long as he kept it in the family. Ken didn't restore the D1, just got it going

Ken Ascott, D1 and friend twice rode Lands End-John O'Groats. (Ken Ascott)

and MoT'd, and did a few long day runs such as the British Two-Stroke Club's Chiltern 100 before deciding to tackle John O'Groats to Lands End.

With fellow club member Don Cannon (making the journey on an MZ) he rode from his home near Peterborough down to Penzance, covering the 370-odd miles in a day. Setting out from Lands End next morning, they reached Tewkesbury on the first night, after negotiating Bath's rush hour in heavy rain. Next morning it was up to Worcester and then Preston to pick up the A6 (they were sensibly avoiding motorways if at all possible) over Shap to Carlisle and the A74, stopping the night near Gretna.

The next day was a hectic one, forced to use the motorway through Glasgow, though they still managed 277 miles before stopping on the A9 near Cromarty Firth. They reached John O'Groats lunchtime next day and stayed "a short time" before heading southwards and home. Three

days ride saw them back home, having covered 1970 miles. The Bantam needed a single chain adjustment and its points cleaning when the bike began misfiring on the overrun. There was also a weep from the fuel tank, which Ken blamed on a pothole that he didn't see until it was too late. Spares were limited to an inner tube, points and a chain link – not that they needed them all.

In fact, the ride went so well that Ken and Don did it again in 2006, to celebrate the D1's 50th birthday. This time they rode north to south, though Don had to make a detour halfway through. Ken carried on alone, reaching Lands End after five-and-a-bit days riding from the other end. He stayed at the famous Lands End Hotel, but was back on the road at 9am next day, for the long haul back to Peterborough – it took him 12 hours!

Proof, if any were needed, that a 50-year-old Bantam and 75-year-old rider were still capable of epic rides.

Ken Ascott's grandson might just make the next generation of Bantam rider. (Ken Ascott)

– she was from Yorkshire, and had ridden from Montreal on her Francis-Barnett, but bought a 197cc James before tackling the Alaska Highway, then 3500 miles of gravel and dirt roads.

Peggy hadn't even taken her test when she bought 'Oppy' (after registration OPE 811), a 1950 D1 Bantam purchased brand new. She celebrated passing with a two-up tour of Somerset (including Porlock Hill) before heading off to Sweden for six weeks. That was two-up as well, with camping gear, and despite rain, Belgian cobbles and a staple diet of fried onions, it gave her a taste for travel. The following April, she shipped Oppy to Canada. As pillion, she had Matelot, a 60lb Airdale pup, who sat in a big box on the luggage rack.

"When I first sighted the Rocky Mountains, I seemed almost to have fulfilled the object of my trip – to journey across Canada from the Atlantic Ocean to the Pacific coast by motorcycle ... It gave me quite a thrill when I considered that this comparatively slim-frame little motorcycle had already carried me over 6000 miles across eight of Canada's eleven provinces. Oppy, my gallant little 125cc BSA Bantam, is used to pulling heavy loads after her Scandinavian tour in 1950, carrying myself and my 160lb Australian girlfriend, plus camping gear ...

"I am very obstinate, and in spite of the warnings was determined to ride through Canada the whole way and not, like the most sensible people, to take the smooth, fast highway through the States."

But she found that a few miles short of the Saskatchewan border the tarmac ran out and ahead lay around 500 miles of gravel roads across the prairies. Typically, she soon got the hang of it: "By the end of that first day on loose surfaces, I felt I could go anywhere and had at last mastered the art of driving over gravel. As long as I steered along the sometimes rather narrow car tracks, and didn't wobble off into the piled up gravel on each side, I could clip along about 35mph; but once off this track Oppy became rather out of hand, and the only remedy was to change down quickly and rev her up out of the skid." Matelot got to know the signs, and would bale out if the Bantam began to go sideways!

But she only came off twice in the entire trip. Once when a bridge was under repair – she fell off at 20mph and was trapped under bike, but a passing workman wouldn't help because he was afraid of getting bitten by the dog! The second time was after an all-night party at her host's

USA, Canada & Mexico – Peggy Iris Thomas

Without doubt, the queen of long-distance Bantamites was Peggy Iris Thomas. In 1951/52, she rode her Bantam 14,000 miles through Canada, the USA and Mexico and the book she wrote, *A Ride in the Sun*, is a travel classic. But she wasn't the only female overlander in those early post-war years; Brenda Collins, a journalist from Kent, did a similar tour by Bantam, and Joan 'Toni' Henley covered 12,000 miles across the US on her B33. Theresa Wallach had co-piloted a Panther sidecar outfit the length of Africa before World War II, and after the war headed across the States on her Norton. Peggy met a woman named Avril near Vancouver

Not a Bantam, but many people took the advice for touring. (Peter Old)

house in Winnipeg. Over a breakfast of spaghetti and tomatoes, she got the urge to get back on the road, having been in Winnipeg for a whole four days.

"I left Winnipeg with some very happy memories. As the morning wore on, I began to feel sleepier and sleepier. The road was smooth, and there were no bumps to keep me awake. Several times my eyes seemed to nearly close."

She stopped for a coffee at Potage La Prairie, where a fellow English traveller insisted on paying for her coffee and introducing her to the whole café, which came out to see her off. "Well on I went, still feeling sleepy. The road stretched out flat and straight, and the sun beat down so that one felt warm and drowsy. Suddenly, before I knew what was happening, I opened my eyes to find Oppy careering down the grassy edge of the road and heading straight for a wheat field! Two very worried American tourists picked me out of the ditch."

Typically, Peggy wrote it off as not being a big deal. She straightened the Bantam's clutch lever and windscreen, "wiped the blood off a small

Weekend green-laning is a more modest Bantam adventure.
(Roger Fogg)

Karachi. Empress Market.

The River Tiber, Rome, showing the St. Angelo Bridge and part of the fortress and the Dome of St. Peter's in the background.

The mountain village of Chateaux D'Oex in the Canton of Vaud, Central Switzerland.

UNX170

BSA

B.S.A. Motor Cycles Limited, Birm
reserve the right to alter designs or any constructional details of their

MC 1008-3.

scratch", and carried on, though she did stop for a good sleep a little way down the road.

Peggy, Matelot and Oppy landed in Canada with just $60, and though she would pick up work where she could find it, she had to travel on a budget in the meantime. Bantams don't drink much, and Peggy appears to have lived on a diet of spaghetti and tinned beans. This got into the papers, and from then on, she was invariably

Exploring off the beaten track was still possible in 2008.
(Roger Fogg)

Karachi, Switzerland, Rome – all within reach of a well-laden BSA. (Peter Old)

offered money, beer and/or food by the people she met. "I shall always remember the two amusing young men who made a date to take me to lunch in Regina. The result next day was the biggest steak I have ever seen in my life. They admitted to having read about my spaghetti and beans diet."

She rode from Halifax to Quebec, then through Ottowa, Niagra Falls, Saulte Marie by the Great Lakes, through Minnesota and back into Canada at International Falls. Then to Winnipeg and across the prairie to Moose Jaw, Medecine Hat and Calgary, over the Rockies to Banff and Vernon, before carrying on to the Pacific. They encountered grizzlies, black bears and chipmunks, and campsites in the Rockies were a boon after wild camping in the prairies, with taps and basins, "instead of a chilly dip in a lake or a scanty scrub-up from my water-bottle!"

A twistgrip problem in Duluth, USA brought the bike to a halt at 10pm in "the roughest looking part of the city". Peggy had only a few cents of US currency, as she was expecting to make the Canadian border next morning, so she phoned the police. They sent out a mechanic, who fixed up a pull string to get her going to the campsite. Next morning, she used the string to ride one-handed

EUROPE ON £15 A MONTH

Was this the motorcycle equivalent of those 'make do and mend' tips so necessary in Austerity Britain? Many Bantam riders really did tour Europe for their summer holidays, but in 1952 came the news that the Chancellor was cutting the foreign touring allowance from £50 per person to £25. The country was still in such dire financial straits that holiday makers were only allowed to take a limited amount of money over the Channel – this had to cover fuel, accommodation, food ... everything. But, as Mollie and Ken Craven explained in *The Motor Cycle*, it could all be done with a bit of careful management.

They spent a month abroad in 1946, covering 3000 miles and spending less than £30 between them. Admittedly they slept in haystacks and barns where they could, and thought that roughing it 'added to the fun.' Petrol was thought pricey at 6s a gallon, and oil quite expensive, but they thought a tenner would buy enough of both for a 2000-mile tour.

You could eat well on the Continent for 7 shillings, but for lunch the Cravens tended to economise by picking up 'hunks of peasant cheeses, tomatoes ... perhaps a few slices of a sausage rich with garlic! We like the simple peasant foods.'

As for hotels, seeing the local working men drinking in the bar was a good sign of its general affordability. The bike would need a good service before setting off, to avoid expensive repair bills eating into that precious allowance. Finally, readers were adviced to put the bike's thirst before their own, and leave enough petrol money to make it back to the ferry!

back into town. It wasn't an easy trip: "my first experience of American heavy traffic ... It was a nightmare, and regulated by eight pairs of traffic lights. Every one of these lights was against me, and each time I slowed down, the engine stalled. The string-pulling just didn't work when I was in first gear, and barely in second, the only alternative was to keep her roaring in top with the clutch slipping. All this was very difficult and the noise was deafening; from every direction people were yelling wisecracks as only Americans can."

She made it to the recommended dealer, only to be told, "We never touch those Limey bikes." Back through the lights again to a second dealer, up a steep hill. The Bantam stalled. She was pushed to the shop by two hefty passers-by, only to find that the shop owner was away in the army, and only there at weekends. His mother tried to help, but salvation came in the form of a visitor who happened to call in, fixed the twistgrip, "and within half an hour I was riding up Main St for the last time, and heading for the Canadian border."

In fact, various bike dealers helped her out. One in Montreal overhauled and cleaned Oppy for free, "and the mechanic gave me a few lessons after I had mentioned that my mechanical knowledge was nil." Another shop in Calgary did a decoke, though she later learnt how to do this herself, but she still had much to learn about Oppy's internals. A friend helped decoke the bike in a dark basement, and the new piston rings went on, 'more by feel than anything else.' Oppy started first kick, but within a day or so had lost all compression. It turned out one ring had been put in upside down.

They fixed that, but putting it back together her enthusiastic friend Bernice managed to snap the gudgeon pin, and there was half an inch missing from one side. 'As the circlip seemed to fit over this OK, we went ahead and finished the assembly job.' Peggy and Bernice went for their usual Sunday ride next day, but she did drop in on a dealer friend on the Monday, to ask if it mattered to ride with a broken gudgeon pin. The horrified Canadian gave her a selection of spanners and a new pin, which she fitted without a problem. Just as well, for the following weekend she rode 150 miles to see friends in Seattle.

After working for the winter near Vancouver, Peggy prepared to hit the road again. 'If I stretch the dollars I have earned this winter, and little Oppy's insides hold together, I hope to tour through the United States and part of Mexico for about three months All is ready ... I have shorts for California, a large sombrero for Mexico, a swimsuit for the Gulf, my sheepskin jacket for the Atlantic coast, and nylons for New York ... I am going about my work singing, 'California, here we come.' The rest can take care of itself when we arrive.'

Riding the Wall of Death – Allan Ford

The Wall of Death has been part of fairground culture since the 1920s, and at one time the roaring wall was a common sight. Now, only a few are left, but they carry on, keeping alive the spirit of riding a motorcycle round a vertical wall, seemingly defying the laws of gravity and delighting everyone who watches.

Allan Ford built up part of his career around

of the show – here, he said, was a local lad having a go. 'I went home and got my Bantam – it was just the most suitable thing I had. I just took the silencer off to make it sound better, and set off. I fell off several times – I couldn't walk very well that week – but by the end of the week I'd cracked it.'

As for the Bantam, the D3 was light, but the plunger suspension wasn't suitable for Wall riding. 'It used to wobble around like a jelly, and I thought there has to be a better way.' Wall of Death riding relies more on lightness and rigidity than sheer power – which is why pre-war Indians are still favourites – so the Bantam was halfway there already. Allan gathered together a D1 rigid frame and a 175 engine. He beefed up the frame, made his own girder forks and added a small fuel tank from an Italian moped. 'I gave it a chopper look,' he later recalled, 'as that was the thing at the time. The bike was superb on the Wall, really easy to ride.'

From then on, whenever he had the chance, Allan would take his Bantam along to the Wall and ride. Eventually, Tommy Messham offered to take him on full-time, and a new career was born. It was the start of a long association with the Wall of Death for Allan Ford, who would eventually buy his own Wall and take it on tour. In the meantime, he toured Europe with Tommy Messham, and the faithful Bantam. A lot of first-time Wall riders made their first tentative rides on that bike, and it was even used successfully on a Globe of Death, a sort of 360-degree version of the Wall that sees bike and rider on an internal 'orbit,' sometimes upside down.

But riding the Wall of Death by Bantam wasn't just down to Allan Ford's love of the little BSA. Tommy Messham liked it so much that Allan built him a replica, and other Wall riders such as Chris Lee also started out on Bantams. Messham stopped using Bantams in the early 1980s, going over to Honda CB200s, which just like the Bantam ten years earlier, had the benefit of being light enough, plentiful and cheap. But that wasn't the end of the story for Allan Ford's Wall of Death Bantam. In the 1990s it was beautifully restored by his friend Kipp Green, and Allan carried on using it for what it did best – riding the Wall of Death.

riding the Wall of Death ... and he started out on a Bantam. Back in 1971, Allan was a young man working at Dan Barrett Motorcycles in Redhill, with a Gold Star that he loved and a D3 Bantam as his ride to work bike. He went to see Tommy Messham's Wall – then the last Wall of Death in operation – at Epsom, and was instantly hooked. Every night during Derby Week Allan went back to watch the stripped down Indians and Suzuki T10s blast around the Wall. But he soon decided just watching wasn't enough – he had to have a go himself.

'I approached Tommy Messham at the end of one evening and asked if I could try it, on my own bike.' Not only did Messham agree, but he seems to have admired Allan's initial attempts to be part

My first Bantam – Philippa Wheeler

"They say you never forget your first love, perhaps it is equally true for your first motorcycle. I was an unlikely motorcyclist, given strong parental

Bantams proved ideal for riding a vertical wall. (Allan Ford)

disapproval ... too dangerous ... too much traffic on the roads nowadays etc. However had I not left home the year before in the face of even greater disapproval to receive the Queen's Shilling and a suit of Air Force blue? So just before Christmas 1958 I bought a ten year old Bantam D1, for £20.

"My first home run on leave started in the gathering gloom of a late January afternoon, much later than intended because of a certain intransigence on the part of the Accounts Section in the matter of pay. I faced 180 miles on the A47 from East Anglia to Birmingham, and how daunting and lonely and far it all seemed as night fell, the wide yellow beam from the headlamp rising and falling with the revs. The fog which enveloped me was freezing, and as my ungoggled eyes ran the tears formed an icy rime round the sides of my Amy Johnson style leather helmet. I fell on the ice for the first time at Hockering, phoned home then fell off thrice in Wisbech. I had never been so cold in my life. Through the long night the little engine never missed a beat, stuttering bravely as I groped my way westwards. Beyond Uppingham the fog cleared and under a starry sky my discomfort intensified as the speed rose and the cold ate malvolently through my two pairs of woollen gloves and civilian mac. The diary records with admirable if surprising precision that I arrived home at 3.12am, after eleven painful hours on the road.

"That first icy ride home was just an unpleasant memory as the winter of 1959 drifted slowly into Spring. That year would see me clock up 12,000 miles in nine months on the D1, much of it wearing a groove at weekends between Norwich and Birmingham. The Bantam could be coaxed up to its 35mph cruising speed with downhills hovering around a blistering 40mph. Not always without incident – the way of the motorcycling novice is hard.

"Still of course in Air Force blue, my days and sometimes nights were spent watching radar screens for Her Majesty. By exchanging shifts with others a quite surprising amount of time off could be accumulated, and once duty ended it was heigh ho and off up the A47 homewards. Thus on a mid-April night I finished my five to midnight watch and set off.

"I was soon speeding towards Kings Lynn, but just short of West Bilney forward motion slowed, though the engine was still running sweetly, a puzzle that seemed to have no obvious solution as I coasted to a stop by a churchyard wall. The moonlight gleamed on the tombstones, the village was in darkness. I felt very alone, even vulnerable and reluctantly I stopped the engine. Of course the lights went out. Direct lighting. By now inspiration had told me that the clutch had failed and while considering what to do next headlights appeared behind me from the direction of Narborough. A taxi which had been taking some lads back to the V bomber base at Marham pulled in behind. The driver considered the matter of the clutch only briefly: there was a garage a mile down the road, Hang on the back of the taxi and I'll pull you along. This novel progress ended in I

L-plates, pillion pad and a massive screen and legshields to keep off that chill Norfolk air.

Philippa Wheeler's D1 (here with a friend aboard) covered 12,000 miles in nine months.

think East Winch and I gratefully settled into the taxi for the few miles into Kings Lynn.

"As part of her general parental advice for offspring setting out into the world Mom had advised that if one found oneself alone and in difficulty, accost a policeman. A brief trudge around the deserted streets took me to the Police station, where the desk officer listened sympathetically to my tale of woe. The Inspector came on at 6am, and provided I was out by then I was welcome to a cell. He would leave the door open.

"Traffic at six o'clock on a Sunday morning in Kings Lynn in the 1950's was not exactly gridlocked, so I walked a good part of the ten miles back to my Bantam. The garage was open by now, the garage man helpful, at first anyway; for I fear I wore my welcome out rather. Remove the foot controls, the gear case, dismantle the clutch and wash the plates free of oil. All this and struggling with the retaining circlip took some time and attracted an audience, free with advice if not with the spannering. The observant reader will no doubt wonder why so much attention was given to freeing a clutch of oil when it was supposed to run in the stuff. The significance was totally lost on me.

"At last it was done, and modestly triumphant I straddled the bike and prepared to apply foot to kick starter. One of the audience cleared his throat and observed in the broadest Norfolk something along the lines of, 'Gor Blarss! Are you not gooin to put the chain on?'

"It was a long walk back along the road to where the chain had disappeared stealthily the previous night. No, I didn't find it. Yes, the long suffering garage man found a box of well matured and rusted old chain that was cobbled together and lasted, miraculously, to Castle Bromwich aerodrome on the outskirts of Birmingham. Then I caught a bus."

Short Way Up* (on a shoestring)
*With apologies to "Long Way Down"

Ewan McGregor and Charley Boorman had brand new R1200GSs, provided by BMW. Neil and I did not. We had a 1968 D14/4 Bantam, and a '53 Francis-Barnett Falcon, whose total cost was about the same as the *Long Way Down* budget on video film. Ewan and Charley had a full-time cameraman on another GS, and two fully-equipped four-wheel drive back up vehicles. We didn't have those either, though Roger and Mignon Fogg did carry our luggage in their Renault Clio. *The Long Way Down* team spent months on proper research and preparation. I fitted a mirror and a new speedo cable to the Bantam – I may also have checked the gearbox oil and the tyre pressures.

We all meet up at Tintern in the lovely Wye Valley, with a simple plan. To ride up through Wales, seeking out some challenging passes on the way and tackle Bwlch-y-Groes, where the original Bantam prototype was tested 50 years ago. Somewhere above the freezing fog, we know there is sunshine, but it seems a long way off as we kick the bikes into life and head up the A466. At least, we do once Neil has cured the flooding carb on his Fanny-B by giving it a sharp tap with a heavy spanner. *Then* we set off. About ten minutes later

D14/4 and Francis-Barnett tackled Welsh passes. (Peter Henshaw)

Setting off from a foggy Tintern. (Roger Fogg)

I realise he has disappeared from my mirror; stop, turn round, and pass him going the other way, giving me a thumbs up. It turns out the Falcon's throttle has stuck open, but now all is well.

Past Monmouth and onto the A40, which commits us to a dull 16 miles of dual-carriageway before getting to the more interesting roads. It seems to take an eternity, and a nerve-wracking one at that, at the Falcon's 40mph crusing speed, as the HGVs rush by. Still, after the Bantam's speedo expires, the actual figure is of academic interest. It goes out with bang though, the needle jamming against the 80mph stop before finally disappearing somewhere in the innards of the instrument. Our next stop reveals that my lovely new speedo cable has tried to twist itself around the rear wheel spindle, but it's not going anywhere, so we carry on.

Eventually (well, it seemed like a long time) we reach the Abergavenny roundabout and lead a convoy of cars up the A465 for a few miles, before turning off onto the Capel-y-ffin road. This is more like it. Away from the traffic, we can potter along the single-lane blacktop at our sedate pace, without anyone breathing down our necks. It's gone 10am, but a hard frost lingers on the verges, and we are still in thick fog. Once clear of Capel y ffin, the climb up to the pass comes all of a sudden, and within a couple of minutes we're in brilliant sunshine. Down below, we can just make out a shepherd, his flock and three sheepdogs, doing a masterclass in sheep management. Looking over the other side of the pass, towards Hay on Wye, the valley is filled with fluffy white fog, but up here there's just bright, clear sunshine.

We creep down into the mist again, and I am reminded that the Bantam needs a new front brake cable. Tea and cake in Hay, where like alcoholics walking past the pub, we avoid all the bookshops and get back on the bikes. That's one thing about riding long distance on small bikes, especially old British ones. They'll do it, but you have to keep the schedule in mind, especially in mid-November. Over the Wye, up the other side of the valley and back into bright sunshine again, though it isn't so much fun riding down Glascwm Hill – it's a toss up between which is worst, the Bantam's over-run lurching, the knackered brake cable or the icy patches that haven't seen any sun today.

We finally hit the main road, and with darkness falling, the temperature plummetting and 70-odd miles to go, decide to stick to it. Neil and I fill up, to find that the bikes have only managed 70-80mpg, which is a bit disappointing. Still, they are crackling on regardless, which counts for a great deal. The Falcon seems happier at 40mph on

Bantam needed all four gears to mount Hay Bluff.
(Peter Henshaw)

Remote filling stations still had two-stroke dispensers.
(Peter Henshaw)

Worth the climb – the view from Hay Bluff.
(Peter Henshaw)

undulating roads, where Neil is able to stay in top (out of three) where I am constantly shifting between third and fourth on the higher-revving, high-compression Bantam.

It isn't late when we reach our B&B at Llanegryn, just beyond Tywyn, but it feels like it – nothing like gritter lorries to make you feel colder and more tired than you really are.

Next day dawns bright and frosty again, but both bikes start promptly – the Bantam will go first kick from cold, so long as you flood the Amal properly, though this takes a very long time. Up the B4405, past the beautiful Tal-y-llyn Lake, before swooping down the A487 with Cadair Idris on our left. Neil claims to have seen 46mph on the Falcon's bicycle speedometer, and the Bantam certainly seems happier the faster we go (within limits).

None of us have ridden up Bwlch-y-Groes before, the highest pass in Wales that kicks off with a 1:4 hairpin. A visiting Englishman named it 'Hellfire Pass' (which was a bit over the top) and Austin test drivers used it in the 1920s, a couple of decades before John Garner arrived here with the prototype Bantam. The D14/4 is soon down to second as we inch up the side of the valley, but it romps up with only slightly more blue haze than usual. Only in the last quarter-mile, do we drop out of the power band, when it's down to first and a 10mph crawl.

I stop at a fork, just short of the top, and hear Neil pull in behind me. The Falcon's made it, but seems to be making a lot of noise. 'Oh,' says Neil, 'the tailpipe's fallen off – thought it was going rather well.' He heads back down the valley to retrieve it; waiting at the top, the rest of us can hear the little Villiers a full minute before we see him, as it hauls the Falcon all the way back up again. Bike and rider are a small black dot near the bottom of the pass, but the sound of the unsilenced two-stroke reverberates off the valley walls.

Then we spend another 20 minutes there while Neil straps his tailpipe and baffles back on again, using a piece of continuous jubilee clip which he just cuts to size – Roger and I are impressed. We've never seen a continuous jubilee clip before.

At the lakeside in west Wales. (Peter Henshaw)

Fanny-Bs break down, too. Neil Sinclair is strapping his silencer back on. (Peter Henshaw)

Bantam and Fanny-B proved (mostly) reliable. (Roger Fogg)

By Tal-y-llyn lake. (Peter Henshaw)

Small two-strokes give every hill climb a sense of achievement. (Peter Henshaw)

Down in Bala, by the lake, there's time for more tea and cake, and Mignon finds a shop that sells chocolate motorbikes. Now the easy thing to do would be to head straight back to the coast on the main road, but the sun's shining and the bikes appear to be running well, so we we ride west into the Snowdonia National Park, through Forestry Commission land on a gated road that has an aversion to following contour lines – it likes to cross them at ninety degrees, whether up or down. The Bantam has developed a bad flat spot at low revs, so the hill climbing technique consists of changing down early and using the D14/4's rev-happy nature instead, while the Falcon chugs up in a high gear, like a little steam engine. That night, over a fine dinner at the Railway Inn at Tal-y-llyn, we decide to do one more pass on the way home next day.

It's signposted out of Machynlleth as the 'narrow mountain road' to Llanidloes, but turns out to be a bit of a doddle. The gradients are steep, but it's a two-lane road with good visibility, so we can take a good run at the hills to give the little two-strokes a fighting chance. Neil and I swap places in a constant battle of torque (Falcon) versus high revving power (Bantam).

Still, with a long way to go south, it's inevitable that we'll have to stick to main roads after Llanidloes. Which we do, and I'm just resigning myself to a long and uneventful ride home when the Bantam starts rattling. It could be the primary chain, or maybe (this is Neil's initial theory) that the slack rear chain is jumping over the gearbox sprocket under load. I tighten the chain – no difference. Neil has a quick go up the road, and

Blue haze as the Bantam reaches the top of a Pass.
(Mignon Fogg)

announces that the rattle isn't there in top gear. So that's that, I'll just have to ride all the way back to Tintern in top, or as much as possible.

Twenty miles later, and not only is the Bantam still going, but it's singing along at 50-55mph, climbing hills in top that would demand third at lower speeds. Only on the long climb out of Talgarth do I need to change out of fourth, though the rattle doesn't get any worse. The clutch doesn't mind a little slipping, and we get through roundabouts and villages, all in top gear – once we're passed Abergavenny, it's as if we're on the home stretch, which we are. Cruising into Tintern 40 minutes later, I'm just congratulating myself and the bike, when the engine cuts out. Surely it can't have failed in the last quarter-mile, after 360-odd up and down mountain passes? There's plenty of fuel, and I'm resigned to pushing, but I give the bike one last prod, and it bursts back into life. We've made it.

Neil and the Falcon arrive half an hour later, but only because he got lost, stuck on the road to Newport and did an extra 20 miles or so. It's not been an incident-free trip, but we've done what we set out to do, and both bikes (the odd rattle aside) are still in one piece, and brought us home. Next year, it's Bantam across the Sahara.

Living with a Bantam

11

Choosing – buying – owning – restoring

So, you may have been inspired by this book and fancy buying a Bantam yourself, perhaps as your first classic bike, or even as your first bike full stop. As a lightweight, cheap-to-run classic, the Bantam certainly has its plus points. It's also a lot fun – for confirmation just talk to any Bantam owner.

However, it's not quite as simple as that. You might buy a decent Bantam and find that you don't like it at all! So, before taking the plunge, it's worth asking yourself a few questions: What sort of riding do you want to do? Are you happy working on the bike as well as riding it (or do you have

a friendly pair of hands to maintain it for you)? Do you want speed, glamour and sex appeal (in which case, keep saving for that Bonneville, and leave the Bantam alone).

As a basic commuter two-stroke with its roots in the 1930s, the Bantam doesn't always fit well into a 21st century lifestyle, and there are several reasons why one might not suit you at all. Firstly, there's the performance, or lack of it. Today we're used to 'twist & go' 125s that can whip away from the traffic lights and cruise at 70mph. A Bantam will not do that, and even the final 12.6bhp D14s and B175s could only manage 65mph flat-out, with leisurely acceleration. The 148cc D3 can just broach 50mph, but the original D1 is even slower, with acceleration to match.

None of this matters if you're pootling around quiet country lanes, and some would say that the limited performance is part of any Bantam's charm. On the other hand, the thought of riding one along a busy motorway, or through manic urban traffic, or trying to cover long distances in a hurry, doesn't bear thinking about. The little BSA was designed for a different world, and expecting one to keep up with today's hectic pace will probably end in frustration or worse.

Secondly, and this particularly applies if you've been riding a modern bike, the Bantam has fairly rudimentary brakes, lights and suspension. Actually, the cable-operated drums were well up to contemporary lightweight standards when they

Anna Finch is 5ft 2in, and fits a Bantam well.
(Peter Henshaw)

106

If the engine's smoking this much, something's amiss
(Roger Fogg)

were new, but for modern traffic, the front brake on a D1, D3 and D5 is quite weak. From the D7 onwards, the cast-iron drum was an improvement, and all Bantams had decent rear brakes, but it's worth bearing in mind if you're used to hydraulic, ABS-equipped discs: ride with anticipation. It's a similar story with lights, though again these improved over the years. Many pre-1966 (and some post-'66) Bantams had direct lighting – i.e. the lights only work while the engine's running, and get dimmer as the revs fall. A 12-volt conversion for battery-equipped bikes is one popular improvement.

As for suspension, the rigid D1 has rudimentary front forks (early models had no damping either) and no rear suspension whatsoever. However, things gradually improved over time, and by the end, the final B175 had a decent swingarm rear end plus Triumph-derived forks, well up to the standards of the time. As with the performance issue, none of this really matters for gentle rides on quiet roads (until you round a blind corner on a country lane to be confronted by a giant John Deere tractor) – once again, it all depends what sort of riding you want to do. And of course, there are dedicated Bantam riders out there who really have done epic trips through modern traffic, so it can be done.

Thirdly, the Bantam is a two-stroke, and not everyone likes these. Some riders like their inherent simplicity, but there's no denying that an elderly two-stroke is noisy, smelly and smoky compared to a contemporary four-stroke in good condition. Two-strokes are prone to uneven low-speed running, and if you care about these things, it's doubtful that a Bantam would get within a sniff of passing today's emissions legislation.

Bantams are slim, simple, and easy to ride.

Some 21st century owners might also get a culture shock when it comes to kickstarting, as all Bantams come from the pre-electric start era, and they have manual, not automatic, chokes. But, as these things go, the Bantam is very easy

Owning a Bantam brings its own reward. (Roger Fogg)

to start, requiring neither bulging thigh muscles nor black art techniques. From cold, it's a case of fuel on, choke on (either the 'strangler' behind the carburettor on early bikes, or the chrome handlebar-mounted lever on later ones) and lightly flood the carb via the tickler button. The bike should then start within three kicks, and if it doesn't, something is wrong.

Finally, and this applies to any older bike, running a Bantam requires care and attention. We've got used to the fact that modern bikes and cars will run between services with only minimal attention in the meantime, often little more than a check of the oil and a chain adjustment. Old machines aren't like that, hailing from an era when most owners did their own basic servicing and

Light weight and small size make these ideal first bikes.
(Roger Fogg)

when all consumer durables (for want of a better phrase) needed more looking after.

Actually, the Bantam is less demanding in this respect than four-stroke classic bikes – there's no engine oil to change every 1000 miles for example, or tappets to adjust. And it's a very simple machine, with little to go wrong, especially in the case of the early D1 and D3. Having said that, it does demand a different mindset to running a modern bike. Riders need to keep an eye on things: is that nut coming lose? Is that the start of an exhaust leak that will only get worse with the miles? If this begins to sound as if you should expect trouble all the time, then it's not like that, but you do need to be sensitive to how the bike is running, and act accordingly. It's called mechanical sympathy, and it applies to any mechanical device that's seen four or five decades of use.

Something else that doesn't apply to modern bikes (even two-strokes) is the need to pre-mix the petrol and oil, as there's no separate tank and pump to do this for you. According to expert opinion, this should be to the ratio of 25:1, so if you've put 5 litres of petrol in the tank, you then need to add 200ml of two-stroke oil. In the Bantam's heyday, many garage forecourts had an oil dispenser that would provide the exact amount (per gallon of course, in those Imperial days) at 25:1, 32:1 or whatever the required ratio. A few garages in the remoter parts of Wales still have them, but at most modern filling stations, you'll have to measure it out of the bottle. Some bottles of two-stroke (inexplicably) have no gradations on the side. Some tank caps have a measuring cup, though of course this relates to buying gallons of petrol, not litres, so it's safer to work things out yourself. Bantams, incidentally, will run quite happily on unleaded fuel and the latest synthetic two-stroke oil.

All these little things are part of Bantam ownership, and some riders of modern bikes would dismiss them as needless hassle. But plenty of Bantam owners would say that they are part of what makes riding one more satisfying than, say, a modern 125cc scooter. You develop a relationship with it that is quite different to that had with a bike that always starts on the button and never goes wrong.

The upside

Now you may have read through the last couple of pages and decided that the Bantam is not for you, but do read on, because they have plenty of positive attributes as well. First of all, size matters, and never more so than with bikes. Modern

Autojumbles are a good source of spares, as long as the seller's reputable. (Roger Fogg)

Not many filling stations have oil dispensers. (Roger Fogg)

two-wheelers seem to get bigger, heavier and taller by the year, and consequently more difficult and initmidating to handle for smaller people,

Bantam parts are generally not hard to come by! (Roger Fogg)

However, the Bantam is a genuine lightweight, small enough for just about everyone to hop on and get both feet on the ground, and not feel in the slightest bit intimidated. That also makes it supremely easy to manoeuvre and park in tight spaces – a Goldwing it is not.

A welcome side effect of the size issue, and especially relevant to anyone looking to buy a Bantam as a second bike, is that its low weight and small size make it easy to tuck into the corner of the garage, and move around as need be. It also makes things easier at restoration time, as the components are correspondingly small and light. Lifting a hefty Bonneville or Commando motor out of the frame is a two-person job, but the complete Bantam engine, gearbox and clutch unit weighs little more than 20 kilos.

Secondly, Bantams are easy to ride. They were designed to be everyday transport, not a challenging weekend toy, as bigger bikes often are now, so they had to be be very easy to use, with light controls and a forgiving nature. And they

or novices. Even some modern scooters can be surprisingly large, with high seat heights that have the shorter-legged teetering on tip-toe at red lights.

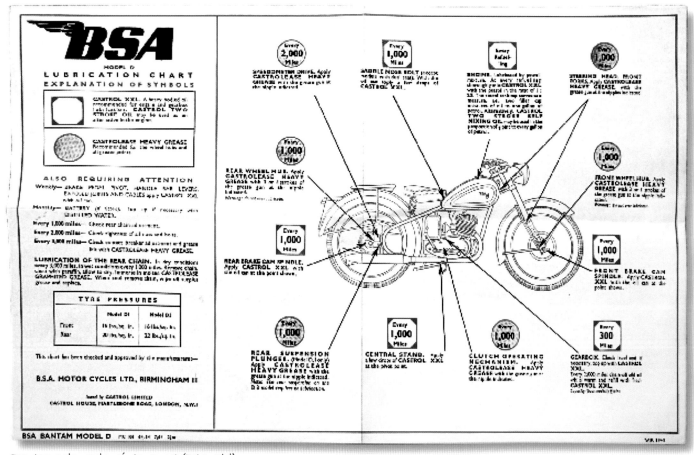

Bantams do need maintenance! (Peter Old)

'2 measures per gallon' translates into 40ml per litre (for 25:1).
(Roger Fogg)

are. Thousands of people learnt to ride on the little BSA, for just this reason. Many owners of big classic bikes also keep a Bantam as a their second classic, and often hop onto that for the local ride to a club night, simply because it's easier than hauling out and starting up the Bonneville or Velo.

Contrary to what contemporary road tests might have said, Bantams do not corner as if on rails, but as long as you watch out for grinding footrests, they have stable and secure handling. They're adaptable too. The Bantam's suitability for trials was discovered very early on, but even the road bikes are quite happy to take on some gentle green laning. This isn't to advocate proper mud plugging, but on a nice dry gravel track, a Bantam should potter along nicely at 20mph or so without offending anyone. If you do come to a dead end, or the going gets sticky, it's very easy to turn it around and head back the other way.

Notwithstanding what we said earlier about limited performance, the Bantam still makes a good town bike, as it's so easy to thread past traffic queues, and to park. Two-strokes have a reputation for being peaky and fussy, but the relatively slow-revving Bantam engine is much more four-stroke in its nature, happy to trundle along at low speeds and less likely to stall than the tempramental two-stroke of popular conception. This applies less to the D10, D14/4 and B175, which were more highly tuned and lost some of that flexible nature.

There's something else that belies the Bantam's modest performance. If you can find the right roads, and are prepared to keep to a 40-50mph cruising speed, then the Bantam can cover big distances. At that 40-50mph, it should happily manage 200 miles in a day, with luggage, though attempting this two-up might be a bit of a struggle. Bantam history is littered with examples of riders who have made epic trips. Early BSA adverts are full of Bantam owners who toured Europe, did Lands End-John O'Groats or crossed Australia or the Alps. And not all of these took place in the 1950s – see page 92 for Ken Ascott's more recent Lands End-John 'O Groats runs.

Touring, or indeed riding anywhere, at these speeds can be a liberating experience. While it's true that Bantam performance can be a liability on busy roads, given the right stretch of quieter tarmac, it becomes a charming asset in itself. Because it's a struggle to keep up more than 50mph up hill, down dale (make that 40 for the D1/ D3), one tends not to bother. At slower speeds, you see more, and it's easier to stop and turn round if you spot a pub/teashop/scenic view that simply can't be missed. Riding more slowly is also less tiring, with less wind chill and noise, so 200 miles isn't as daunting as it sounds, even if it does take longer. Because dull motorways are effectively out of bounds, you have to seek out more interesting roads. And if you don't want to go long distance touring, a Bantam could help you discover some enjoyable small roads local to home that you would miss on a big modern bike.

Practicalities

Now some people buy a classic bike for its rarity, but that doesn't arise with the Bantam, apart from particular models like the early Competition, or the later Sports or Bushman. BSA made over 400,000 Bantams, and it's thought that about half of these still exist, whether as boxes of bits or complete running bikes. So, there are plenty to choose from, and they often come up for sale. If a suitable Bantam doesn't appear straight away, be patient, because something that suits you should be along before too long.

Finally, Bantams have another huge advantage compared to many other classic bikes – they are very cheap to run, which, given their background as basic, everyday transport is hardly surprising. Power and performance might be limited, but it does wonders for the life of tyres, brakes and chains – tyres can last up to 20,000 miles.

A Bantam in the attic? Unrestored examples still turn up. (Roger Fogg)

supply a specific part, may be able to suggest an alternative: they are listed in the appendices, and all details were correct at the date of publication. Do beware of buying cheap parts of unknown provenance on eBay – genuine spares are so affordable that there's not much point in doing this anyway.

Motorcycles need insurance (even if you're planning to just keep your Bantam in the garage as a keepsake) and the news here is good, too. Bantams aren't worth a fortune, and don't cost much to repair, while their performance is some way from the superbike class. Consequently, insurance doesn't cost an arm and a leg. In the UK, all pre-1973 vehicles are exempt from road fund duty, which happily includes all Bantams.

Nor will you spend much on fuel. Bantams might have relatively dirty emissions by modern standards, but they make up for that with fuel consumption of around 100mpg. In fact, as powered transport goes, the little BSA has quite a small carbon footprint. Apart from the modest thirst, all Bantams are old enough to have written off their manufacturing emissions.

Spares are cheap, too, and most parts are readily available. A few spares are getting tricky to find, but many more are being remanufactured in batches, for the very good reason that with so many bikes surviving, there's a big market out there in Bantam spares. Even new, genuine BSA stock sometimes turns up as well, because Small Heath churned out mountains of spares as well as complete bikes. Many lay dormant on dealer shelves for decades, being sold off as job lots whenever they had a clearout. As icing on the cake, there are some very knowledgeable Bantam specialists in the UK, who, even if they can't

There's one other thing about Bantams that is a definite advantage and makes them very enjoyable bikes to own. Honda might have coined the phrase about meeting the nicest people on one of their bikes, but it applies just as much to the BSA. It's worth repeating that for a couple of generations of UK teenagers, a Bantam was their first bike, with all the memories of a misspent youth that that entails. So whenever you stop to buy fuel, or outside the newsagents or just about anywhere, somebody (usually middle-aged or older) will come up to you with a broad smile, saying, "I had a Bantam just like that!" As well as the countless thousands who once rode a Bantam, there are thousands more who still do; enthusiastic, friendly people who will welcome you as a fellow 'Bantamite'. Details of the thriving owners club are in the appendices.

So, whether or not you can happily live with a Bantam depends on the sort of riding you want to do. As a 40-plus-year-old commuter

The proverbial basket case should be the makings of a complete bike. (Roger Fogg)

Check engine mounts are secure and not cracked. (Roger Fogg)

This D7 is almost complete ... (Roger Fogg)

bike, built down to a price when it was new, the performance, braking, lights and suspension are pretty basic. But as a rewarding, cheap-to-run classic with a charm all of its own, there's a lot to be said for a Bantam.

Where to find one

As noted earlier, finding a Bantam is not difficult, as there are lots of them around, at least in the UK and certain parts of Europe, and there will always be a selection for sale, whatever time of year. The Bantam was also widely exported, and though by comparison there are few bikes in the USA or Australia, they do exist. In fact, the Aussies have a long history with the little BSA, from sheep farmers using them as farm bikes to the Bantam racing scene that used to thrive down under.

In the UK, keep an eye on the classified ads of *The Star* (the BSA Owners Club magazine) and *Banter* (of the Bantam Owners Club) – you'll need to join, but this is a good idea anyway, as it gains access to the helpful community of active Bantam owners. There's also the *VMCC Journal*, *Old Bike Mart* and, on the newsagents' shelves, *Classic Bike* and *The Classic Motorcycle*, which carry adverts from dealers as well as private sellers. Dealer stocks turn over regularly, especially in the spring and early summer, so it's well worth keeping an eye on the dealer websites which are (or should be!) updated as soon as new bikes come in.

While on-line, there's always eBay, where there's usually a selection of Bantams on offer. Even more so than with buying a bike through more traditional methods, it's a case of *caveat emptor*. Some buyers will happily bid for a bike

Buying at auction could deliver a bargain. (Roger Fogg)

Want a restoration project? There are plenty of candidates.
(Roger Fogg)

without viewing it, but it's still worth a journey to assess the bike properly before bidding. You will have to be quick though, as the eBay world moves fast. Make use of the 'seller's history' section to check up how the seller has treated previous customers, and many dealers make use of eBay. It's also not unknown for bikes for sale to be 'ghost' machines which don't really exist, or not in the form they are advertised. You could still pick up a bargain through eBay, especially if there's little interest in the Bantam you're bidding for, but pre-bid viewing is still strongly recommended.

Finally, though less popular now thanks to the convenience of on-line buying, there are auctions. Specialist motorcycle auctions are still held up and down the UK, with prior notice in the classic bike magazines. Although you'll need to make a special journey to attend one, and may come home empty handed, prices are usually lower than those asked by a dealer or private seller. On the other hand, there's only a limited opportunity to inspect the bike, and you won't be able to test ride it. The golden rule, as for any other auction selling anything, is to decide in advance what your maximum bid will be, and stick to it – it's all too easy to get carried away on the day, and end up paying over the odds. If you make a successful bid, the bike becomes your responsibility straight away, so you'll either have to insure it and ride it home or have a bike trailer on hand.

AUCTIONEERS
Bonhams www.bonhams.com
Cheffins www.cheffins.co.uk
eBay www.ebay.com
H&H www.classic-auctions.co.uk
Palmer Snell www.palmersnell.co.uk
Shannons www.shannons.com.au
Silver www.silverauctions.com

Restore, or ready-to-ride?
Buying a Bantam offers the complete range of motorcycle purchase experience – that is, everything from the familiar autojumble basketcase (a collection of well worn and rusty parts that may or may not add up to one complete bike) to a concours machine, built to a standard better than new.

This is a starting point, but be prepared to search for missing parts. (Roger Fogg)

Which one suits you best depends on a great many things, but the money available is an obvious one, as is your time, inclination and skills with regard to undertaking a complete restoration. There's an undeniable romance about restoration projects, about bringing a sick bike back into blooming health, and it's tempting to buy something that 'just needs a few small jobs' to bring it up to scratch. But there are two things to think about: one, once you've got the bike home and start taking it apart, those few small jobs could turn into big ones; two, restoration takes time, which is a precious thing in itself. Be honest with yourself – will you get as much pleasure from working on the bike as you will from riding it?

If you don't want to restore the bike yourself,

then the obvious alternative is to hand over the whole thing to a professional. But be warned, the cost will never, ever be covered by the increased value of the bike. Ultra-rare and sought-after bikes like the BSA Rocket Gold Star will always be worth restoring professionally, because there are so few genuine ones around and they fetch sky-high prices. That's obviously not so with the Bantam. Impeccably restored bikes are of course worth a lot more than tatty ones, but never enough to cover the astronomical cost of professional restoration.

You may still decide to go this route if you have the budget and/or don't have the time to do the job yourself. If so, there are several issues to bear in mind. First of all, when talking to the restorer, be absolutely clear what you want done. Do you want the bike to be simply roadworthy and useable, or 100 per cent original, or better than new? There's a whole debate surrounding the merits of 'ultimate restorations' that leave a Bantam far shinier and built to a better standard than it ever was at Small Heath. This approach will win show awards and (hopefully) involve superb workmanship. On the other hand, it's out of kilter with what the Bantam was originally about, and having spent that much on the bike, you might be reluctant to take it out on the road.

Whatever level of restoration you ask for, get a detailed estimate that is more or less binding. Restorers will understandably only want to give such an exact figure once they've dismantled the bike and worked out exactly what needs doing. Also check that the company you're dealing with has a good reputation – the owners club, or one of the reputable parts suppliers, should be able to make a few recommendations. If their name is good, then expect to go on a waiting list – a good restorer will have a steady flow of work that cannot be rushed.

If you do decide to do most or all of the work yourself, there's good news, as the Bantam is a very easy bike to work on. Of course, restoring one still requires a certain level of skill, and it does help if you have a warm, well-lit garage with a solid workbench and a good selection of tools. There's no lack of literature on looking after the Bantam. The Haynes manual is still available new, while copies of the original BSA workshop manual and instruction manual, and the *Pitman's Book of the BSA Bantam*, all come up at autojumbles. Have a think about what skills you have, or would

like to acquire. Can you weld, or paint? Are you confident with electrics or major engine work?

As noted earlier, the good thing about the Bantam is that its small size and simplicity gets you off to a flying start. And of course it is easy to work on anyway. One Bantamite told the author that for gearbox jobs, he could have the engine out of the frame, crankcases split, and gearbox repaired within an hour! Not everyone will manage that, but the Bantam's engine in particular is very simple, and it is true that the only special tools needed to take apart the entire engine/gearbox/clutch – in other words, the whole bike – are a flywheel puller

... and one day it could look like this. (Roger Fogg)

115

Chewed-up fasteners are a sign of previous owners' abilities! (Roger Fogg)

Once the engine is apart, it's always worth replacing the primary chain, gearchange selector spring and crankshaft seals, even if they appear to be OK – none of them cost much, and replacing them at a later date will involve taking the engine down all over again. While you're there, a complete set of engine bearings is also cheap, so if there's any doubt about the originals, replace those too.

Although all this work is relatively easy, do take note of the order in which the various spacers, seals and washers go, so that they slip straight back in, in the right order. This applies to wheel bearings as well as the engine/gearbox unit. The frame shouldn't need any repair work apart from blasting and repainting, though the long through bar on D1/3/5s which makes up the footrests is often bent. On a well worn bike, the centre stand will usually need new feet welded on – complete new stands are available as well, and it's well worth fitting a side stand, for convenience. These were an option when the Bantam was new, so it's a viable original fitting.

and clutch compressor, though a clutch-locking tool (home-made by brazing an old pair of friction and plain plates together) is useful as well. The crankcases should come apart easily, and if they don't, it's likely that not all the connecting screws have been taken out – many Bantams have gouged crankcase joint faces, where previous owners have attempted to prize the cases apart with a screwdriver! If it needs that much force, something is wrong.

Finally, Bantam electrics don't have the best reputation, and these have to be reliable. New wiring looms are available, and well worth fitting to any bike that has been standing for some time, or has generally unreliable electrics. All connections, especially earths to the frame, must be clean and tight. Electronic ignition, if the bike doesn't already have it, is another big improvement, taking out the contact breaker points and making for better, cleaner starting and running. The change is also invisible from the outside, so doesn't upset the original appearance.

All of this work, other commitments permitting, should be easily achievable over a winter rebuild. But if you've bought your Bantam in the spring, it can be frustrating to see the summer pass before you even get a chance to ride it. A rolling restoration is one answer. Ultimately, it will take longer than doing everything in one go, but it means you get to ride the bike in the meantime, as well as spreading the cost over a longer period. That's not the way to achieve a concours finish,

A professional respray does give good results. (Roger Fogg)

which can only really come after a complete nut-and-bolt rebuild, without the bike getting wet and gritty in the meantime. As ever, it all depends what sort of experience you're looking for: riding, the rebuild experience itself, or a show winner?

Alternatively, you could forget all the above and just a buy a bike that's ready to ride. Even if its not concours, you should get a lot of fun out of it straightaway. And if after a few months you've found that the Bantam experience is worth pursuing, that's the time to take the bike off the road for a while and attend to the cosmetics.

Which one?

Over a 23-year production run, the Bantam changed considerably. The basic layout was much the same in March 1971, when the final Bantams left the line, as in 1948, when the first ones did, but in the meantime power nearly trebled, the gearbox acquired four speeds, there were better lights, alternator electrics and a swingarm frame with decent front forks. These changes came gradually, over the years, so it is possible to pick and choose which Bantam will suit you best.

Of course, some think that the final B175, with all those changes, was the best Bantam of all, with the best performance, best suspension and most powerful electrics, but it's not quite as simple as that. Others will say, with just as much conviction, that the best Bantam to buy is the original D1, as it's the simplest and lightest, with least to go wrong. Although the D1 rigid or plunger Bantam is still available in big numbers, it also fetches the highest prices, and when restorers do choose a Bantam for a complete nut-and-bolt rebuild, they tend to focus on this one. What follows is not a directive about which Bantam you should buy, but a look at the strengths and weaknesses of each model so that you can decide for yourself.

One interesting point is that this sharp distinction between different models of Bantam, their engine sizes and exact specification, can be somewhat artificial. While it was all true when the bikes were new, a lot may have happened to a machine in the 40-odd years since. Although things did change, many Bantam parts are interchangeable between different models. Any engine for example, will fit any frame, and it's just about possible to fit any fuel tank as well. This offers the prospect of, say, a lightweight D1 rigid frame with a late 175 engine and four-speed gearbox. More relevant to the point of view of buying a Bantam, it's more than likely that the engine/gearbox and other parts will have been swapped over the years. At one time, it was quicker and cheaper to find a second hand

engine at a breakers' yard than repair the existing one, so owners often did just that, bolting it straight in. So if you want an original bike, the same spec as it left the factory, make a careful inspection, with particular reference to engine and frame numbers (see below) which will tell you the model provenance of the power unit and cycle parts, and whether they have a common ancestry or not!

Prices go up and down, so instead of quoting actual prices, there's a percentage quoted here, which shows how the model values vary in relation to each other – The D10, D14/4 and B175 are used as the 100 per cent baseline. Although rarer models such as the D1 Competition, the Bushman and D10 or D14/4 Sports will fetch higher prices if original and in fine condition, generally prices are more dependent on condition than model. Having said that, D1s are generally worth more than the others, and D7s the least. The final 175s, despite having all the desirable developments, and being thought by some to be the most practical Bantam of all, are priced no more than average.

In terms of availability, the most common Bantam to appear on sale is the D14/4, closely followed by the D1. There are fewer D7s available, considering their long production run, but it's understandable that few D10s come up, as they were only in production for a year. Relatively short production runs also restrict the availability of D3s, D5s and the final B175s.

Bantam D1/D3 1948-63

The original BSA Bantam D1, launched at the Earls Court Motorcycle Show in 1948, was the most basic of the breed. If you buy one of these you really will be owning a machine with its roots in the pre-war era. It was the D1 that bore most resemblance to DKW's RT125 on which it was based, but having unit construction and a foot change gearbox, it was by no means outdated for its time.

The 123cc two-stroke produces 4.5bhp, which when the bike was new allowed a top speed of 47mph, with 35-40mph cruising. There was a three-speed gearbox, and the engine came with basic Wipac magneto electrics, direct lighting and no battery. All of this was slotted into a simple welded frame with rigid rear end and undamped forks that relied on grease rather than oil for lubrication. Not surprisingly, the original D1 provides the most basic Bantam riding experience of all. It's the slowest of the bunch, though also the lightest, and as noted, some Bantamites prefer the D1 to the later, more complicated Bantams. In the familiar Mist Green and cream colour scheme, it's the iconic Bantam for many people, with a quality look eluded by the rather dull looking D7 and flashy Sports and D14/4.

This is the plunger D1 that was ridden by Ken Ascott from Lands End to John O'Groats, both ways. (Ken Ascott)

over the decades. The factory bike had a modestly upswept exhaust, a decompressor in the cylinder head, raised saddle and footrests, a folding kickstart, bigger rear sprocket (for lower overall gearing), non-valanced mudguards and roller front wheel bearing. Unfortunately, it didn't have a specific engine or frame number coding, so you have to rely on those accessories to pinpoint one – the decompressor is a giveaway.

From 1950, the roadster D1 also had the option of Lucas battery electrics, which were offered for three years. These brought coil ignition and battery lighting, though purists maintain that it's simply more to go wrong. The Lucas system was dropped in 1953, when a battery-based Wipac system became optional. The same year as the Lucas electrics, Bantam buyers could also pay extra for plunger rear suspension. With just 3 inches or so of movement, these don't make a huge difference, but do add some comfort.

In 1954, the D1 Bantam was joined by the 148cc D3 Bantam Major, now with 5.3bhp and a top speed of just over 50mph. The bottom end was beefed up to suit, and the main bearings were now partly lubricated via a feed from the primary drive. It looks superficially similar to the D1, but the D3 has its filler cap on the right instead of the left (also adopted by D1s) and didn't have the D1's gear indicator near the gearbox sprocket. Another recognition point (apart from the frame number)

All the comments about lack of performance, weak lights and brakes apply most strongly to the D1, but it does offer the purest Bantam experience of simplicity in the extreme.

One D1 variant well worth looking out for is the Competition. This was launched for 1950, and aimed directly at trials riders who were already discovering that the lightweight Bantam, with its tractable engine and nimble manners, made an excellent trials bike.

The challenge of course, is in differentiating a genuine D1 Competition from the countless home brewed Bantams that were converted to trials spec

is the Pastel Grey and cream colour scheme on the tank, in place of the D1's Mist Green. Like the D1, it came in battery or direct-lighting form, or as a Competition, though the plunger frame was standard and it had rubber damping in the front fork (which the D1 also adopted). A swingarm frame replaced the plunger in 1956, though the D1 plunger soldiered on, and, in fact, would last until 1963, thanks largely to GPO orders.

Strengths: These early Bantams are the simplest of the lot. So they are extremely light (especially the rigid frame D1) and easy to work on. D1s, despite being in production for 15 years, are more sought after than D3s.

Weaknesses: All D1s/D3s have limited performance for busy modern

Somewhere behind that large fairing is a D7 Super. (Roger Fogg)

roads, with only adequate brakes and electrics. The post-1955 swingarm D3 is more comfortable, but heavier, blunting the performance of the 148cc motor.

D1: 120 per cent
D3: 117 per cent

Bantam D5/D7 – 1958-67

Launched in autumn 1957, the D5 Super Bantam brought the 174cc engine size that would stay with the bike for the rest of its production life. With 7.5bhp, it brought significantly better performance – a top speed of close to 60mph, with 50mph cruising – along with a caged-roller big-end bearing and, to cope with the extra urge, slightly wider brake shoes. It kept the D3 swingarm frame and wide-ratio three-speed gearbox but added a more bulbous two-gallon fuel tank.

Today, the D5 is quite rare, because it only lasted a year before being replaced by the D7 Super. Opinions are divided on the D7. According to the late Bob Currie, the well known motorcycle journalist who must have tested most if not all varieties of Bantam, the D7 was the best compromise of the lot, with a comfier swingarm frame than the early bikes, but the mild 174cc engine less 'revvy and peaky' than the later more highly tuned 4-speed Bantams. That's the positive view. Others damn the D7 for being neither one thing or the other, lacking both the D1's charming lightweight simplicity and the later bikes' real-world performance. And at 232lb, it was the heaviest Bantam yet.

Not only did the D7 retain the D5 (and for that matter D1/D3) three-speed gearbox, but this was actually weakened, thanks to a modification to the mainshaft splines. So, a gearbox originally designed to cope with 4.5bhp was now expected, in weakened form, to manage 7.5! Inevitably, there were failures, though it's likely that any D7 around now will have long since been there, done that, and hopefully been upgraded with the later stronger mainshaft.

The D7 did bring some worthwhile changes as well, notably more effective cast-iron (not pressed steel) brakes and oil-damped forks, while with its headlamp nacelle and smoother styling the D7 looked a bit like a BSA Thunderbolt in miniature. Meanwhile, the 174cc engine was usefully torquey and flexible. Despite which, the D7 remains something of a Cinderella among Bantams. Memories of the troublesome gearbox are probably partly to blame, plus the fact that it's not as 'pure' a Bantam as a D1. Despite a long production run of eight years, the D7 changed little, evidence that BSA was neglecting Bantam

development at the time, in favour of its export-friendly big twins.

If the standard D7 Super looks a little dowdy, look out for the De Luxe from 1964, with the slimmer kidney-shape fuel tank that would become a Bantam trademark to the end, and chrome panels, Flamboyant Red paintwork and ball-ended levers. Unfortunately, it was still hampered by the same wide-ratio three-speed box. A cheaper option was the D7 Silver, with minimal chrome plating and direct lighting.

Strengths: Significantly extra performance over the D1/D3, with improved brakes to match on the D7. D5s are rare, but the D7, in production for seven years, is still relatively easy to find. In 7.5bhp form, the 174cc engine is understressed. More comfortable, with more effective forks than earlier bikes. D7 is the most affordable Bantam, D5 less so, thanks to its rarity.

Weaknesses: Hampered by wide-ratio three-speed gearbox, which was weakened on D7. Electrics are no better than on earlier bikes, and both D5 and D7 lack the lightweight charm of an early Bantam.

D5: 115 per cent
D7: 88 per cent

Bantam D10 – 1967

In 1967, with the D10, BSA appeared to be trying to make up for seven years of neglect, and the latest Bantam brought some significant changes. Power was boosted by the best part of 40 per cent, to 10bhp, thanks to a higher compression, a bigger carburettor and other changes, which brought a top speed up to a true 60mph. From the D10 on, Bantams have a fighting chance of keeping up with modern traffic. An easy recognition point (apart from the engine number) is the pancake air filter. The three-speed gearbox was strengthened to suit, now back to its original format of two sets of splines on the mainshaft and layshaft, though this still wasn't always enough to cope with the big power boost, and its wide ratios were brought into sharper relief by the engine's peaky delivery. Just as significant, the old direct lighting and Wipac generator was finally ditched in favour of a crank-mounted 60-watt alternator.

Optimistic about the revamped Bantam, BSA expanded the range with the new D10 Sports and Bushman, which had no more power than the cooking Bantams but did come with a new four-speed gearbox, which proved more reliable than the three-speed. The Sports was aimed at aspirant coffee bar cowboys, and the Bushman was one of the first dual-purpose trail bikes. Both models are now quite rare, though they do come up for sale

Just the thing to impress your mates outside the local caff. (Roger Fogg)

now and again, and only 300 Bushmen stayed in the UK – the rest were exported to Australia, New Zealand and Africa. When looking at a Bushman, as with the Sports or Competition, check that it's a genuine item, and not a common or garden D10 fitted with the appropriate parts.

The more basic Bantams were the cut-price Silver and flashier Supreme, both sticking with the three-speed gearbox. These too don't often appear, as the D10 range was only in production for a year.

More powerful the latest Bantam might be, but the engine was quite different in character to earlier bikes. It needed to be revved to bring out

that extra performance, and that in turn brought harshness and vibration. And while the new alternator gave brighter lights, it could overcharge the system.

Strengths: Extra performance, with an easy 50-60mph, and alternator electrics are generally a step forward. D10 Sports and Bushman are rarities, and sought after.

Weaknesses: Harsher engine loses the softer edge of earlier Bantams; three-speed gearbox still an obstacle to performance; alternator can overcharge; watch out for fake Bushmen and Sports.

100 per cent

D14/4 Supreme flanked by more exotic machinery at a bike event. (Roger Fogg)

D14/4, B175 – 1968-71

The final series of Bantams were the fastest, and in many ways the most sorted, with the best brakes and forks, while the old three-speed box was finally dropped. The D14/4 signified yet another power boost, with a 10:1 compression, bigger ports and exhaust pipe plus fatter compression discs on the flywheels. It all added up to 12.6bhp (not 14, as the name suggested), with near-60mph cruising and good hillclimbing ability, thanks to the now proven four-speed gearbox. A good recognition point is that the chrome pancake air cleaner gave way to a paper element hidden behind the right-hand side cover.

The range was simplified, with the cut-price Silver dropped, and all the D14/4s gained heavier duty fork stanchions, while the Bushman and Sports had rubber fork gaiters, which looked a little snazzier. D14/4 Sports have a slotted one-piece heat shield for the high-level exhaust.

As with the D10, the extra get up and go of the D14/4 didn't come for free, and this most highly strung of factory Bantams was prone to vibration if all the performance was called for. More seriously, the compression discs were now riveted to the flywheel, and these could come loose before letting go in spectacular fashion. This was cured in the final months of D14/4 production. From February 1969, the discs were held more securely by a rolled-in rim lock – look for the engine number prefix 'BC' to signify this.

BSA may have recognised that the D14/4 was a little over-tuned, for the B175 that replaced it in April 1969 had a lower compression of 9.5:1. A B175 engine (or cylinder head at least) is recognisable by its centrally-mounted sparkplug – all other Bantams have the plug canted backwards. Or you might have found a bike with a rare aftermarket cylinder head. As well as the lower compression, the last Bantam benefited from a stiffer crank with bigger crankpins, and what is generally thought to be the best front forks fitted to a Bantam at the factory, based on thosed of the Triumph Sports Cub and with rubber gaiters. The B175 also marked a change from Whitworth to Unified threads.

The Sports and Bushman B175s didn't survive for long, both being dropped in October 1969, while the basic B175 carried on as the lone bike in the range. Colours were black, Flamboyant Red or Flamboyant Blue. It looked very similar to the D14/4, but as well as the central sparkplug, the fork gaiters and 'Bantam 175' badges on the side panels mark it out.

Strengths: More performance for modern traffic; standard four-speed gearbox; on B175, strengthened bottom end and slighty milder engine, plus good Triumph-derived forks. D14/4 Supreme is plentiful and easy to find. Bushman and Sports worth seeking out.

Weaknesses: More performance means more vibration, especially on D14/4; lacks laidback feel of earlier Bantams; alternator electrics can still overcharge.

Points to look for

So you've decided that you really do want a Bantam, which model will suit you best and after hopefully not too much searching, you've found one that sounds like the sort of thing you're looking for. Confronted with the actual bike, what points should you look for? Bantams (and I may have mentioned this before) are simple, uncomplicated bikes, but it still pays to give any potential purchase a good examination before parting with cash. A lot of what follows would apply to any second hand bike, though some of it is specific to the Bantam. However confident you feel about buying/selling, it doesn't do any harm to take a friend along when looking at the bike, for a second opinion. And if you're not, then having someone knowledgeable with you is a real help.

All the usual advice about buying a bike applies. When phoning in advance, try to ascertain whether the person on the other end is a private or trade seller. Arrange to meet at their premises/home, not in a lay-by or motorway services halfway between the two of you. As for paying, Bantams are not expensive bikes, so it

Check engine number ... (Roger Fogg)

... and that on the frame. (Peter Henshaw)

might be worth taking cash along and making an offer.

ENGINE/FRAME NUMBERS

Engine and frame numbers are good clues as to what model of Bantam you're looking at, and when it was made, and these should be the first things you look at. The engine number is located on top of the crankcase, on the left-hand side, but the frame number moved about. It's on the front engine mounting plate or the downtube on D1s, on the headstock on D3s, D5s and early D7s, and back on the engine plate for all Bantams from late D7s onwards.

Use the engine/frame number chart in the appendices of this book. That will confirm what year the bike engine and frame were built, and the BSA Owners Club holds despatch records, which will tell you when this particular bike left the factory.

However, engine/frame numbers aren't infallible. Since any Bantam engine will fit any frame, engine swaps are common, so you could well be looking at a '68 engine in a '59 frame. And unlike, for example, a Triumph twin, not all BSA Bantams left the factory with matching engine/ frame numbers. They tended to start the model year in synch, but this soon went out of kilter as engines were diverted to other markets. Some variants such as the Bushman will have specific frame numbers to confirm that it's a genuine bike. Again, check the chart in the back of this book for details. If the bike comes with an original buff logbook, then this will say what engine/frame the bike had when it was new.

Even if the engine/frame numbers indicate that the bike is a mixture of parts, that's not necessarily a bad thing, as long as you're not a stickler for originality. The bike will never be worth

as much as an all-original example, but it may still be a perfectly good, functioning motorcycle. Finally, whatever engine and frame numbers the bike has, check that they match that on the documentation.

PAINT/CHROME

Bantams didn't come in a huge variety of colours, but these range from the classy (Mist Green and cream D1) to the slightly dull (black D7) to the outright flash (Flamboyant Red D14/4 Sports). If the paintwork is original but faded, there's a lot to be said for leaving it as it is, with its patina of age intact. But if the bike does need a respray, that'll be expensive. You may want to tackle the simple colours yourself, but the later metallic Flamboyant range is tricky to apply properly. Look for evidence of quick and cheap resprays. The correct colour

Professional resprays look great, but are not cheap. (Roger Fogg)

Replating chromework can be expensive. (Roger Fogg)

Faded original paint can make for a pleasant patina.
(Roger Fogg)

for each year is listed in the appendices – paint availability shouldn't be a problem, as there are often modern car shades that give very close equivalents.

As for the chrome, there's not a great deal on the Bantam, though generally BSA added more as the years went by, culminating in the Sports, with its chrome rims, headlight, tak panels, exhaust heat shield, lower fork ends and mudguards. Minor blemishes and dullness can be polished away, but otherwise you're looking at a replating bill.

TINWORK
Tinwork – tank, mudguards and side panels – are often the most difficult parts to replace, though some are being remade now, but if a bike for restoration has everything present and correct, that's a plus. Check that all of these, including the headlamp nacelle (except Sports) are free of rust and dents, and are securely mounted to the bike.

The fuel tank needs to be checked for leaks around the tap and along the seams as well, and watch out for patches of filler. Tiny pinhole leaks in the tank can be repaired with Petseal, but anything more serious needs a proper repair, which means removing the tank and thoroughly flushing it out first. New tanks are available (though they're not cheap), so a very poor condition tank is a good bargaining lever, especially as it's such a focus of the bike's appearance.

BADGES/TRIM
Missing badges and transfers can nearly all be replaced, as apart from the BSA badge on the tank, reproductions of specfic model transfers are

available direct from the BSA Owners Club and the Vintage Motorcycle Club, or via the spares specialists. Even the Sports' chequered band along the fuel tank is still available. Beware that tank badges from an unknown source may not fit exactly!

SEAT
A tatty and torn seat can really detract from the bike's appearance, and it's very easy to replace,

Replacement transfers are available. (Roger Fogg)

Even this could be restored, although new ones are available. (Roger Fogg)

Dual seats can be repaired, recovered or replaced. (Roger Fogg)

rust, and you'll have to do it by feel, as the seat has to be unbolted – it doesn't hinge up. Torn or split covers can be replaced by a specialist, and corroded pans welded back into shape.

RUBBERS

Worn rubbers – on the footrests, kickstart and gearlever – aren't an infallible sign of high mileage, as on a bike this old they're liable to have been replaced at least once already. Either way, footrest rubbers should be secure on the rest and free of splits, and if the footrest itself is bent upwards, that's a sure sign that the bike has been dropped at some point. Beware a worn smooth

Kickstart rubber must be secure. (Roger Fogg)

Footrest rubber wear is an indication of mileage. (Roger Fogg)

so many have been, but for originality, this should be correct for the model. The D1 and D3 had a solo saddle with optional pillion pad, while a dual seat was standard from the D5 Super onwards – export Bushmen had a solo seat as well. The dual seats were usually black with white piping, while the Sports had an all-black seat with a racing hump at the rear end. Another key appearance item, something else that varied from year to year and model to model.

If the seat looks tired, check the metal pan for

Check that frame fixings aren't cracked or bent. (Roger Fogg)

Centre stand is a weak point. (Roger Fogg)

rubber on the kickstart, as you're foot's liable to slip off while kicking the bike over, with painful results as the lever slams back into your leg. The rubber should be firm on the lever and not drop off after half a dozen kicks, though if the engine needs that many kicks to fire up, then something's wrong there anyway.

FRAME
A frame that is really shabby necessitates a strip down and repaint, though as with the other paintwork, if it's original and fits in with the patina of the bike, then there's a good case for leaving it as it is.

A more serious check is whether it is straight and true. Look for signs of a front end impact around the headstock and on the test ride, check that the bike runs straight and steers well. Any serious waywardness should be obvious. The Bantam used three basic types of frame – rigid, plunger and swingarm – all of them simple, straightforward tubular steel designs that spring no surprises.

STANDS
A well worn centre stand will be obvious. It will be at an extreme angle, will be awkward to use and leave the bike resting on both wheels. The rear wheel should be clear of the ground. Eventually the stand's feet wear away,

Don't expect modern 12-volt lighting power from this. (Roger Fogg)

especially if the bike has been started on the stand, which can have it hopping backwards, scraping the stand along the tarmac. New feet can be welded on, but it's an awkward job. When on the stand, the bike shouldn't lean or wobble.

A side stand was optional, and these are readily available, and well worth fitting, as it's easier to use and saves wearing out the centre stand.

LIGHTS
Bantam headlights might be a bit feeble, but they should flick on without hesitation – flickering suggests poor contacts either in the switch or

An LED rear bulb is a good investment. (Roger Fogg)

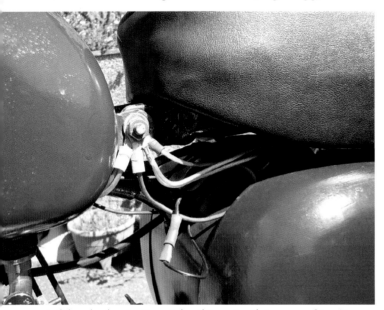

Wiring is simple, though is still a potential source of trouble.
(Roger Fogg)

wiring. On a D1, D3, D5 or D7 with direct lighting, the lights will only work when the engine's running. Check the brakelight – the Bantam had a rear brakelight switch only, but in the UK this is legal for this age of machine. Some early bikes didn't even have one of those, so they'll need one, but new, fairly unobtrusive pull switches are available. A worthwhile modification is an LED rear/stop light bulb, a straight swap for the standard bulb, assuming it fits under the lense, which takes only minimal power but won't blow, leaving you taillight-less on a dark night.

ELECTRICS/WIRING

BSA tried to cut costs on the Bantam, and nowhere was this more obvious than than in the electrics, and a combination of cheap components and outmoded systems (many Bantams used direct lighting right up to 1966) make this a weak spot. The Wipac flywheel generator system will give trouble if not maintained, but if the bike starts promptly, then at least the ignition side of things should be well. If it will only run with a points gap of less than the specified 0.015in, then the generator's rotor needs remagnetising.

From the D10 on (1967) that was ditched in favour of a 60-watt alternator system, which is better all round, though it does have poor voltage control, which can lead to battery boiling through overcharging. The exception was the Bushman, which used energy transfer ignition and AC lights. Battery acid stains on the chain guard or rear mudguard are a sign that the battery has been overcharged. Modern voltage regulators, or a complete 12-volt conversion of this system, offer the prospect of brighter lights and even indicators.

Is the wiring neat and tidy, or flopping around? The bullet connectors and all earths need to be clean and tight for reliability. Check that everything works: lights, horn (not that the bulb-horn fitted to D1s and D3s needs any help from a generator) and brakelight.

WHEELS/TYRES

Wheel condition is often overlooked, but all the spokes should be present, correct and well tensioned – give each one a gentle tap with a screwdriver to check. All Bantams from 1954 on had chrome rims, and replating this involves rebuilding the wheel.

Tyres should be to at least the legal minimum, which in the UK is at least 1mm of tread depth across at least three-quarters of the breadth of the tyre. Many Bantams get used as second bikes (or even worse, half-forgotten at the back of the garage) and may sit unused for months or even

*Tyres may have set hard with age – new ones aren't expensive.
(Roger Fogg)*

All except the early Bantams had chrome rims. (Roger Fogg)

years. Tyres deteriorate, especially if the bike's weight is on them, and will eventually harden and lose their grip, even if they have plenty of tread. Try sticking a fingernail into the rubber – if it's too hard, the bike needs a new set of boots.

<u>WHEEL/STEERING HEAD BEARINGS</u>
These ball bearings aren't expensive, but fitting them is a hassle, and play could affect the handling. To check the front wheel bearings, put the steering on full lock and try rocking the wheel in a vertical plane, then spin the wheel and listen for rumbling. Do the same for the rear wheel. To check the steering head bearings, swing the handlebars from lock to lock; they should move without a hint of roughness or stiff patches. Then check for play by grasping the bottom of the forks and trying to rock them back and forth, though play here could also be in the forks themselves.

<u>SUSPENSION</u>
The Bantam illustrates the complete evolution of motorcycle suspension in the post-war years, from the D1's rigid rear end and rudimentary telescopic forks to the B175's stronger oil damped forks and swingarm rear. The plunger rear suspension optional on the D1 and D3 offers only limited movement, but rarely wears out, making the handling wayward when it does, but new bushes are cheap.

Swingarm rear suspension (standard on all but the basic D1 from 1956 onwards) is more comfortable, but the swingarm bushes need

Wheel bearing check. (Roger Fogg)

checking. The Metalastick rubber bushes fitted to the D3 Major and D5 don't often wear out but aren't that rigid to start with. The D7 onwards used conventional steel-backed bronze bushes, a more rigid set up that works well as long as owners make use of the grease nipple – if not, they're easier to replace than the rubber bushes. To check for wear, get hold of the rear end of the arm on one side and try rocking the complete swingarm from side to side. There should be no perceptible movement.

D1/3/5 forks relied on grease rather than oil as a lubricant, but once again, it's just the bushes that need replacing as long as the forks aren't accident damaged. One point to watch on the D7 fork is the lower bush, which was held in position by centre punching. This could come loose, and would then get rammed to the bottom of the fork, from where it was almost impossible to extract. On all forks, with the front brake on, pump the forks up and down – they should work smoothly without clonking or squeaking. To check for play, try rocking the forks back and forth. Leaks from the hydraulic forks or rear shocks should be obvious, and lack of damping at the back suggests that the shocks are out of oil altogether.

INSTRUMENTS

Checking that the speedo works obviously has to wait for the test ride – if nothing is working, the cable is the most likely culprit, but if either mileometer or speedo have ceased to function, but the other is still working, then there's something wrong internally – instrument repair is best left to a specialist. Several of these advertise in the classic motorcycle magazines, and they can repair and recondition a speedo, keeping the original mileage reading. A battered and bent bezel suggests that a previous owner has had a go themselves.

ENGINE

Take a general look around the engine/gearbox. Chewed up screws or rounded off bolts are signs of

Above: The Bantam's engine is fundamentally robust. (Roger Fogg)

There should only be a faint haze of blue smoke from a warm engine that is not under load. (Roger Fogg)

Speedo repair is a specialist job, but it may just be a snapped cable. (Roger Fogg)

Clean, leak-free, nicely restored engine. (Roger Fogg)

less than skilful previous owners. The two mounting plates must be completely solid, with no missing or loose bolts – if they are, the bike is not in a rideable condition. On the front plate, look for signs of welding repair where the plate may have fractured in the past.

Oil leaks are less of an issue for the Bantam than for four-stroke classics (there's no engine oil, of course) but some unburnt oil may find its way out of the exhaust joints. Gearbox oil may leak from the primary drive cover and gearbox sprocket seal housing. A few drips aren't a problem, but a serious leak needs attention. While you're down there looking for leaks, check the gearbox oil level on the dipstick on top of the gearbox, or the level hole on some bikes, and check the state of the oil itself – nice and clean, or dirty sludge?

Bantams are not hard to start, but while some will go first kick, others need two or three. If starting takes a lot of kicking, or simply doesn't happen, then the first thing to check is the plug. Thanks to modern two-stroke oils, these don't foul up like they used to, but they still get a harder time than plugs in a four-stroke. So take a new spare, and if the owner's agreeable, try that instead.

The recommended plugs are Champion L7 on D1 to D7, or N4 on D10 onwards. The NGK equivalents are BP6HS and B7ES respectively. Points trouble is another cause of poor starting and running, which could be a simple and cheap thing to put right, or

There may be a dribble of burnt oil from this joint. (Roger Fogg)

could be main bearing wear upsetting the timing. Another cause of poor starting, on post-1957 bikes (see below) is a failed crankshaft seal.

It has been known for Bantam engines to start and run backwards, often after stalling, but this is very rare. If the engine hasn't been started since being rebuilt, then it will have to be bump started, and when it does go, there will a lot of smoke in the first five minutes or so.

If you're used to the quiet thumping of a healthy four-stroke, then the Bantam's low-pitched ring-ding-ding may come as a culture shock, but knocking or rumbling from the bottom end means that the main and/or big-end bearings are worn. Replacing these is the biggest single mechanical expense a Bantam can demand, but it still won't break the bank.

Other bottom end problems are less easy to spot in advance, such as loose flywheel plates, which can actually keep spinning after the engine has stopped, evidenced by a whirring sound. This is potentially more serious on the high compression D14/4, where the riveted on plates can let go at speed, causing mechanical mayhem inside the crankcase. D7 engines can snap the end of the crank, but 40-odd years on, it's likely that original faults like these will have been solved. With the engine idling, look back at the silencer and blip the throttle. You should expect a faint haze of blue smoke, as this is a total-loss two-stroke, but there shouldn't be clouds of the stuff once the motor has warmed up with the choke/strangler off. Excessive smoke has a number of potential causes, the most serious of which is a failed crankshaft seal on post-'57 bikes. That sucks gearbox oil into the crankcase, hence the smoke. Remove the gearbox oil filler cap while the engine is running – if you

This battery case may have been damaged by leaking acid. (Roger Fogg)

can see bubbles, that confirms it. Lots of smoke could also be caused by worn or sticking piston rings, though it could just be that the seller has added too much oil to the fuel mix, or has even left the choke on!

PRIMARY DRIVE
Listen to the primary drive while the engine is running. Rattles from this area suggest that the primary chain needs replacing, as it's not adjustable. You won't know for sure without taking the primary drive cover off – if it already is off, and the chain has more than three-quarters of an inch (about 20mm) of free play, you need a new one.

CHAIN/SPROCKETS
Is the chain clean, well lubed and properly adjusted? The best way to check how worn it is is to take hold of a link and try to pull it rearwards away from the sprocket. It should only reveal a small portion of the sprocket teeth. If the sprocket teeth have a hooked appearance, or if any are damaged or missing, then that needs replacing, along with the gearbox sprocket. On some Bantams, the rear sprocket is riveted on, and these will need grinding off, though 'Bantam John' offers a button-head screw conversion, which makes things easier.

BATTERY
You have to unbolt the seat to check the battery on later Bantams (even the D14/4, which has an alleged 'access hole'). Bikes with direct lighting don't have a battery. If you can get to it, check the battery for acid splashes (a sign of

Check the chain and sprockets for wear. (Roger Fogg)

Silencer should be free of dings, rust and leaks. (Roger Fogg)

A test ride is essential. (Roger Fogg)

overcharging). The correct electrolyte level is a good sign of a meticulous owner, and do check that the battery is securely kept in place by its rubber strap, and that the battery carrier hasn't been corroded by acid over the years.

EXHAUST

Check that the exhaust downpipe is secure in the cylinder barrel (looseness causes air leaks) and examine all joints for looseness and leaks, which in the UK are MoT failures. The silencer itself should be secure, firmly mounted and in solid condition. Replacements are available.

Lots of smoke combined with lethargic performance could be a sign that the exhaust needs a decoke. This used to a regular ritual of two-stroke ownership, though it's less of an issue with modern, cleaner burning two-stroke oil. If it needs doing, it's a messy business, but giving the the silencer a good clear-out will be worthwhile. Post-'54 bikes had removable baffles, which makes things easier.

TEST RIDE

However carefully you've examined the Bantam in question, there's no substitute for a test ride. This should be for not less than 10 minutes, and you should be doing the riding – take your driving licence, in case the seller wants to see it, and leaving the vehicle you arrived in is an article of faith that you won't ride off into the sunset on the seller's pride and joy.

If you've never ridden a Bantam before, or indeed any older bike, then take time to acclimatise. Better still, do you have a friend or acquaintance who already owns one that's in

Will a Bantam suit you? (Roger Fogg)

decent nick? If so, try to blag a short ride – that way, you'll know what to expect. Compared to a modern two-stroke, the Bantam is low revving and (especially pre-D10) extremely tractable and forgiving. Don't expect modern levels of performance, though the D10, D14/4 and B175 do have a power band and rev more freely. They are also happy to keep up 50mph, which isn't too far off the pace of main road traffic on major roads. Don't abuse the bike, but don't be afraid to use what performance there is either.

Whatever model it is, any Bantam should pull cleanly through the rev range without hesitating or misfiring, but expect some 'four-stroking'

The clutch shouldn't slip or drag. (Roger Fogg)

Gears should engage cleanly and the lever should return smoothly. (Roger Fogg)

and uneven running when the motor's cold or running slowly. If there is a misfire, and the bike started promptly and isn't blowing out clouds of smoke, then an ignition fault or partially blocked carburettor are the most likely culprits, both relatively simple to put right, but also good bargaining counters. On the other hand, if the bike seems suspiciously slow (compared to that

practice ride you had on your friend's Bantam), and is difficult to start, then it's probably low on compression thanks to general wear.

GEARBOX/CLUTCH OPERATION
While on your 10-minute test ride, check that the gearbox and clutch are working as they should. Don't be fazed by a long-travel gear lever that demands you take your foot off the footrest – they all do that. Gears should engage cleanly, first time, and neutral should be easy to find at a standstill. The three-speed gearbox on D7s and some D10s is a potential weak spot – even if it seems fine, ask the seller if any work has been done here. The three-speeder isn't over-stressed on early low-power Bantams, and the later four-speed box rarely gives trouble. If the gearbox on a D1 jumps out of second, the usual cause is a worn selector mechanism, though persistent jumping out of gear is a sign of impending trouble, whatever the model.

One more thing about Bantam gearboxes, and this affects all of them. If the gearchange is floppy, and the lever doesn't return to the middle position, it may still be possible to change gear, but there's a big job

The gearbox may leak oil. (Roger Fogg)

on the way. It means the lever's return spring has snapped. This is a simple, cheap component, but getting to it involves splitting the crankcases, so it's not a 10-minute job.

The Bantam clutch is pretty bulletproof, and it shouldn't slip or drag if it's in good condition. Click into first from a standstill – is the bike trying to creep forwards, and the engine close to stalling? Then the clutch is dragging. Adjustment should be enough to cure it.

Unusually for an older British bike, the Bantam's primary kickstart drive allows it to be kickstarted, clutch in, when in gear. If it won't do this, then the clutch is slipping, something that will be obvious on the test ride anyway. The clutch doesn't feel that precise, and may engage late, but it's generally tough and gives little trouble so long as the mechanism is well greased.

HANDLING

Despite what pipe-smoking road testers wrote in the 1950s, no Bantam will corner as if it's on rails, unless it's a well set up racer circulating Silverstone, and ridden by someone who knows what they're doing. And when you think about it, that's hardly surprising when you consider the ingredients: skinny tyres (often the cheapest money can buy); fairly basic suspension; and non-folding footrests that will forcibly limit ground clearance even if the tyres allow you to lean that far.

But let's not get this out of proportion. One of the Bantam's attractions when it was new was a proper motorcycle-style tubular frame, with decent-size wheels, so it handled a good deal better than a contemporary Vespa or Lambretta. Even today, a Bantam with decent suspension and tyres should be safe and secure, and any extreme waywardness points to worn shocks, plungers or forks, wheels out of alignment or worn steering head bearings. Wrong tyre pressures can have the same affect, so do check those as well, and if the bike's been sitting in the back of a garage for some time, the tyres will almost certainly be on the squashy side, unless the seller has thought to pump them up.

Even in good condition, the earliest D1 rigid Bantam has fairly crude front forks and no rear suspension at all, so it won't cope with mid-corner bumps as well as a modern machine (or a later Bantam, for that matter). The D1/D3's plunger rear end gives 2-3 inches of movement, which is an improvement, though if the plungers are worn through lack of grease, that can upset

If the brake lever pulls right back to the bars, a new cable and/or brake shoes are needed. (Roger Fogg)

the handling – the bushes are relatively easy to replace. Finally, the swingarm Bantams won't handle as they should if the rear shocks are out of oil and/or the swingarm bearings are worn.

The D7's hydraulically damped forks were a great improvement on the earlier grease-filled set-up, but better still were the D14/4 forks with thicker stanchions. Best of the lot were the 1969-71 forks on the B175, taken from the Triumph Sports Cub. You will have already checked the forks for leaks – on the test ride, they shouldn't bottom out with a clonk over potholes, or judder when you brake.

Cable condition, not just the brake itself, affects stopping power. (Roger Fogg)

BRAKES

A lot of words have been written (some of them in this chapter) decrying Bantam brakes. The truth is that they were acceptable by commuter bike standards of the 1950s and early '60s, and in good condition, they should be capable of bringing the bike to a halt fairly quickly – the rule of thumb is within 30 feet from 30mph.

However, they can still leave something to be desired in modern, fast moving traffic, and this is especially true of the pressed steel drums fitted to the D1, D3 and D5. The cast-iron drums (D7 onwards) are better, and were based on those of the Tiger Cub. In both cases, the rear brakes are generally better than the fronts. If the front lever comes back close to the bars, the brake needs relining and/or a new cable. 'Sponginess' also indicates it's time for a new cable. On the test ride, you may need to acclimatise to the brakes as well as everything else, especially if you've just climbed off a modern bike. The author remembers testing a D14/4 immediately after riding a whizz-bang BMW with servo-assisted ABS brakes. By comparison, the Bantam's front drum appeared to be lined with pig fat rather than friction material, but over time I realised that it wasn't too bad.

CABLES

All the control cables – brake, throttle and choke – should work smoothly without stiffness or jerking. Poorly lubricated, badly adjusted cables are an indication of general neglect, and the same goes for badly routed cables. Note that even new looking cables may not be best quality.

SWITCHGEAR

Switchgear is simple in the extreme. There's no ignition key (apart from on the rare D1 De Luxe) and you normally get just an ignition switch, lighting switch, plus a combined horn/dip switch on the bars. The exact configuration depends on which model you're looking at. This was one of the many areas in which BSA pared costs on the Bantam, and the Wipac switches aren't particularly well made or positive, but they should work

Tired cables mean less efficient brakes. (Peter Henshaw)

Some bikes have an ignition switch here as well. (Roger Fogg)

the lights/horn/ignition reliably. Malfunctioning switches are usually a simple problem to solve, but another reason to bargain over price.

REGISTRATION/MOT
The following specific information applies to UK legislation, but wherever you are, in order to be road legal your Bantam will need to be registered, and pass a roadworthiness test. If the bike is already up and running, with a current V5 document and MoT, then all well and good – you can put this book down and ride happily off down the nearest stretch of tarmac.

But life isn't always so simple. Back in the early 1980s, the old buff logbooks were replaced by the V5, and all vehicle registrations were transferred to the DVLC and its infamous computer. (You don't hear so many DVLC computer jokes these days, either because the big beast makes fewer mistakes, or because most people have a PC sitting on their desk at home, so 'computers' have lost their sinister Big Brother-ish overtones).

Anyway, the Bantam you've bought and/or restored may not have been on the road since that momentous change, either because it's been sat mouldering in someone's shed for the past quarter-century, or was reduced to a box of bits long before the change came in. Or it may have had its identity legally stolen – in other words, the registration number has been bought as a personalised plate to satisfy the vainglorious whimsy of a motorist.

Whichever of these is the case, the bike will have to be re-registered. There was a time when DVLC insisted that re-registered vehicles could only be issued with a 'Q' plate, which looked a little naff on a 1959 Bantam, or for that matter anything old and classic. They've since relented, and will provide an age-related plate that looks right on the bike. And if the bike's original registration can be traced (via the engine/frame number) and no one's nabbed it in the meantime, then you can even use that.

However, you do need to prove that the bike exists, and really is the age you are claiming it to be. Fortunately, the BSA Owners Club in the UK will provide a dating certificate from the original factory dispatch records. You'll need to send it a whole sheaf of documentation to support your claim, including pictures of the bike, rubbings of the engine and frame numbers, the old logbook,

A currently registered, road legal Bantam should come with V5C and MoT documents. (Peter Henshaw)

Bantams are road tax exempt in the UK, but still have to display a disc. (Peter Henshaw)

any old MoT certificates and tax discs, plus any other evidence of the bike's age. Also include forms V55/5 and V765, duly completed. If all this tallies, and the BSAOC identify the bike's true age from the despatch records, they will forward the whole lot to DVLC, who will check it all and (hopefully) approve the granting of an age-related plate.

In the meantime, get the MoT and insurance sorted out, using the frame number to identify the bike. Contact your local Vehicle Registration Office, explaining what you're intending to do, and send them the complete V55/5, dating information from BSAOC, MoT and insurance documents, plus the fee. If the VRO are happy with all of this (and they should be, after all the trouble you've been to) then they will issue an age-related number. Job done!

MoT
To avoid wasting time and money on a failed MoT test, check the bike over yourself before booking the test. Check that all the lights work, and that the reflector is good and shiny; if the Bantam doesn't have a rear brakelight, fit one. Check the forks, steering head bearings and (if applicable) swingarm bearings for wear. Are the chain and sprockets in good condition? The handlebars should swing freely from lock to lock without snagging or binding the cables. It goes without saying that tyres will have more than the legal minimum tread, and will be free of perishing and

splits – watch for the latter on bikes that have been standing for a while. If there's any doubt about the brake linings or cables, fit new ones.

One other thing. Ask a fellow Bantam (or other classic bike) owner where they get their machines MoT'd. Why? Because some testers will rarely, or never, have come across a bike of the Bantam's age, and compared to the modern machinery they're used to testing, its lights and brakes will seem feeble, let alone the bulb-horn fitted to direct lighting D1s and D3s. A tester used to classics will understand that these components are as good as they can be, but they certainly won't pass anything that isn't safe.

Appendix 1: model profiles

D1 – 1948 to 1963

Bore x stroke	52 x 58mm
Capacity	123cc
Compression ratio	6.5:1
Power	4.5bhp @ 5000rpm
Electrical system	Wico-Pacy flywheel magneto, direct lighting
Generator output	30 watts
Battery capacity	N/A
Ignition timing	0.15625in BTDC
Points gap	0.015in
Sparkplug	Champion L7
Carburettor type	
D1 1948-50	Amal 261/001D
D1 1951-63	Amal 361/1
Choke size	0.625in
Carburettor settings	
Main jet	75
Slide no.	5
Needle position	2
Petroil ratio	20:1
Clutch friction plates	3
Gearbox ratios	
1st	22.1:1
2nd	11.7:1
3rd	7.0:1
Suspension	
Front	Telescopic fork, coil sprung, undamped (rubber damped from 1954)
Rear	Rigid (plunger optional from 1950)
Brakes	
Front	Drum, 5 x 0.625in
Rear	Drum, 5 x 0.625in
Wheel & tyre sizes	
Front	2.75-19 & WM1-19
Rear	2.75-19 & WM1-19
Sprocket teeth	
Engine	17T
Gearbox	15T
Clutch chainwheel	38T
Rear chainwheel	47T
Chains	
Primary size	0.375 x 0.25in
Primary length	50 pitches
Rear	0.5 x 0.305in
Rear length	117 pitches (rigid)
	123 pitches (plunger)
Capacities	
Fuel	1.75 gallons
Gearbox	0.75 pints
Suspension	Grease as required
Dimensions	
Wheelbase	50.5in
Seat height	27.5in
Ground clearance	4.75in
Overall width	26.5in
Weight (dry)	153lb
Exhaust system	Low level
Colours	Mist Green, cream tank panels lined in red and gold. Maroon winged BSA logo. Piled arms logo on toolbox with 'BSA Cycles' script
Saddle or dual seat	Sprung saddle
Notes	The first production Bantam, launched at Earls Court Motorcycle Show November 1948. Rigid frame powered by

123cc petroil two-stroke engine with three-speed gearbox and telescopic forks. Speedometer was listed as extra (though a legal requirement) and fork gaiters were added after the first production batch. Wico-Pacy Geni-mag fitted to August 1950, then Wico-Pacy Series 55/Mark 8. Plunger rear suspension optional from 1954.

D1 Deluxe – 1950-52

Bore x stroke	52 x 58mm
Capacity	123cc
Compression ratio	6.5:1
Power	4.5bhp @ 5000rpm
Electrical system	Lucas alternator, coil ignition, battery lighting
Generator output	watts
Battery capacity	5 amp/hour
Points gap	0.015in
Sparkplug	Champion L7
Carburettor type	
D1 1948-50	Amal 261/001D
D1 1951-63	Amal 361/1
Choke size	0.625in
Carburettor settings	
Main jet	75
Slide no.	5
Needle position	2
Petroil ratio	20:1
Clutch friction plates	3
Gearbox ratios	
1st	22.1:1
2nd	11.7:1
3rd	7.0:1
Suspension	
Front	Telescopic fork, coil sprung, undamped
Rear	Plunger
Brakes	
Front	Drum, 5 x 0.625in
Rear	Drum, 5 x 0.625in
Wheel & tyre sizes	
Front	2.75-19 & WM1-19
Rear	2.75-19 & WM1-19
Sprocket teeth	
Engine	17T
Gearbox	15T
Clutch chainwheel	38T
Rear chainwheel	47T
Chains	
Primary size	0.375 x 0.25in,
Primary length	50 links
Rear	0.5 x 0.305in
Rear length	123 links
Capacities	
Fuel	1.75 gallons
Gearbox	0.75 pints
Suspension	Grease as required
Dimensions	
Wheelbase	50.5in
Seat height	27.5in
Ground clearance	4.75in
Overall width	26.5in
Weight (dry)	153lb
Exhaust system	Low level
Colours	Mist Green, cream tank panels lined in red and gold. Maroon winged BSA logo. Piled arms logo on toolbox with 'BSA Cycles' script
Saddle or dual seat	Sprung saddle
Notes	De Luxe D1 fitted with standard plunger rear suspension and Lucas electrics, including coil ignition and DC battery lighting. Ammeter in headlamp shell is recognition factor. Coil located under fuel tank, rectifier between battery and toolbox. Different crankshaft with heavier flywheels and special outer cover – crank not interchangeable with that of standard D1. Otherwise specification the same as standard D1.

D1 Competition 1950 to 1956

Bore x stroke	52 x 58mm
Capacity	123cc
Compression ratio	6.5:1
Power	4.5bhp @ 5000rpm
Electrical system	Wico-Pacy flywheel magneto, direct lighting
Generator output	30 watts
Battery capacity	N/A
Ignition timing	0.15625in BTDC
Points gap	0.015in
Sparkplug	Champion L7
Carburettor type	Amal 361/1
Choke size	0.625in
Carburettor settings	
Main jet	75
Slide no.	5
Needle position	2
Petroil ratio	20:1
Clutch friction plates	3
Gearbox ratios	
1st	27.10:1
2nd	14.50:1
3rd	8.65:1
Suspension	
Front	Telescopic fork, coil sprung, undamped (rubber damped from 1954)
Rear	Rigid (plunger optional)
Brakes	
Front	Drum, 5 x 0.625in
Rear	Drum, 5 x 0.625in

Wheel & tyre sizes
Front — 2.75-19 & WM1-19
Rear — 3.25-19 & WM1-19

Sprocket teeth
Engine — 17T
Gearbox — 15T
Clutch chainwheel — 38T
Rear chainwheel — 58T

Chains
Primary size — 0.375 x 0.25in,
Primary length — 50 pitches
Rear — 0.5 x 0.305in
Rear length — 117 links (rigid)
123 links (plunger)

Capacities
Fuel — 1.75 gallons
Gearbox — 0.75 pints
Suspension — Grease as required
Dimensions
Wheelbase — 50in
Seat height — 29in
Ground clearance — 7.0in
Overall width — 26.5in
Dry weight — 166lb
Exhaust system — Upswept
Colours
Saddle or dual seat — Sprung saddle
Notes — D1 Competition aimed specifically at trials riders, and the few changes were all made with this in mind. Mechanically similar to the road going D1. Changes included upswept exhaust, decompressor in the cylinder head, folding kickstart, unvalanced mudguards a 58T rear sprocket, lower internal gear ratios, thicker upper fork stanchions and roller bearing front axle. According to one source, it didn't have lights, but 1950 catalogue clearly shows these fitted. D1 Competition was available in both rigid and plunger form.

D3 Major 1954 to 1957
Bore x stroke — 57 x 58mm
Capacity — 148cc
Compression ratio — 6.4:1
Power — 5.3bhp @ 5000rpm
Electrical system — Wico-Pacy flywheel magneto, direct lighting
Generator output — 30 watts
Battery capacity — N/A
Ignition timing — 0.15625in BTDC
Points gap — 0.015in
Sparkplug — Champion L7
Carburettor type — Amal 523/7
Choke size — 0.6875in
Carburettor settings
Main jet — 90

Slide no. — 5
Needle position — 3
Petroil ratio — 20:1
Gearbox ratios
1st — 22.0:1
2nd — 11.7:1
3rd — 7.0:1
Suspension
Brakes
Front — Drum, 5 x 0.625in
Rear — Drum, 5 x 0.625in
Wheel & tyre sizes
Front — 2.75-19 & WM1-19
Rear 2.75-19 & WM1-19
Sprocket teeth
Engine — 17T
Gearbox — 15T
Clutch chainwheel — 38T
Rear chainwheel — 47T
Chains
Primary size — 0.375 x 0.25in,
Primary length — 50 pitches
Rear — 0.5 x 0.305in
Rear length — 123 links (plunger)
121 links (swingarm)

Capacities
Fuel — 1.75 gallons
Gearbox — 0.75 pints
Suspension — Grease as required
Dimensions
Wheelbase — 51in (swingarm)
Seat height — 29.5in (swingarm)
Ground clearance — 4,75in
Overall width — 26.5in
Weight (with 1gal fuel)
217lb (plunger)
228lb (swingarm)
Exhaust system — Low level
Colours — Pastel Grey, cream tank panels, 'Bantam Major' tank transfers, 'BSA Motorcycles' piled-arms transfer on toolbox. Maroon and Black options.
Saddle or dual seat — Sprung saddle, optional dual seat (plunger), standard dual seat (swingarm)
Notes — Bantam Major bored out to 148cc for 5.3bhp and top speed of just over 50mph. New cylinder barrel with larger fins, bigger transfer ports, heavier flywheels, uprated big-end, new two-fin silencer with removeable baffles. Filler cap swapped from left to right-side of fuel tank. Direct lighting standard, battery lighting optional.

D3 Competition 1954 to 1956
Bore x stroke — 57 x 58mm
Capacity — 148cc
Compression ratio — 6.4:1

Power	5.3bhp @ 5000rpm
Electrical system	Wico-Pacy flywheel magneto, direct lighting
Generator output	30 watts
Battery capacity	N/A
Ignition timing	0.15625in BTDC
Points gap	0.015in
Sparkplug	Champion L7
Carburettor type	Amal 523/7
Choke size	0.6875in
Carburettor settings	
Main jet	90
Slide no.	5
Needle position	3
Petroil ratio	20:1
Gearbox ratios	
1st	27.1:1
2nd	14.45:1
3rd	8.64:1
Suspension	
Front	Telescopic forks
Rear	Rigid or plunger
Brakes	
Front	Drum, 5 x 0.625in
Rear	Drum, 5 x 0.625in
Wheel & tyre sizes	
Front	2.75-19 & WM1-19
Rear	2.75-19 & WM1-19
Sprocket teeth	
Engine	17T
Gearbox	15T
Clutch chainwheel	38T
Rear chainwheel	58T
Chains	
Primary size	0.375 x 0.25in,
Primary length	50 pitches
Rear	0.5 x 0.305in
Rear length	123 links (plunger)
Capacities	
Fuel	1.75 gallons
Gearbox	0.75 pints
Suspension	Grease as required
Dimensions	
Wheelbase	50in
Seat height	29in
Ground clearance	7.0in
Overall width	26.5in
Weight	–
Exhaust system	Upswept
Colours	Pastel Grey, cream tank panels, 'Bantam Major' tank transfers, 'BSA Motorcycles' piled-arms transfer on toolbox
Notes	Made in small numbers, rigid or plunger frame. Mechanically similar to road going D3 Major, with 5.3bhp 148cc engine plus the same cycle part changes as on D1 Competition

(decompressor, folding kickstart, upswept exhaust etc) and lower gearing.

D5 Super 1958 only

Bore x stroke	61.5 x 58mm
Capacity	174cc
Compression ratio	7.4:1
Power	7.4bhp @ 4750rpm
Electrical system	Wico-Pacy flywheel magneto, direct or battery lighting
Generator output	30watts
Battery capacity	11 amp/hour
Ignition timing	0.15625in BTDC
Points gap	0.015in
Sparkplug	Champion L7
Carburettor type	Amal Monobloc 375/31
Choke size	0.875in
Carburettor settings	
Main jet	140
Pilot jet	25
Slide no.	3.5
Needle position	2
Petroil ratio	20:1
Gearbox ratios	
1st	20.2:1
2nd	10.74:1
3rd	6.5:1
Wheel & tyre sizes	
Front	3.00-18 & WM1-18
Rear	3.00-18 & WM1-18
Suspension	
Front	Telescopic forks
Rear	Swingarm, twin shocks
Brakes	
Front	Drum, 5 x 0.875in
Rear	Drum, 5 x 0.875in
Sprocket teeth	
Engine	17T
Clutch	38T
Gearbox	16T
Rear wheel	46T
Chains	
Primary size	0.375 x 0.25in,
Primary length	50 links
Rear size	0.5 x 0.335in
Rear length	121 links
Capacities	
Fuel	2 gallons
Gearbox	0.75 pint
Dimensions	
Wheelbase	52in
Seat height	31in
Ground clearance	5.5in
Overall width	26.5in
Weight (with 1 gallon fuel)	

	228lb	Rear size	0.5 x 0.335in
Exhaust system	Low level	Rear length	121 links
Colours	Bayard Crimson (maroon) or	**Capacities**	

Black, ivory tank panels with 'Bantam Super' script, chrome-plated strip on tank seam.

		Fuel	2 gallons (Super)
			1.9 gallons (De Luxe)
Saddle or dual seat	Dual seat	Gearbox	0.75 pint
Notes	The first 174cc Bantam,	**Dimensions**	

using similar cycle parts to D3 Major. Cylinder barrel studs moved out to 60mm to make room for large-bore barrel. New 2-gallon fuel tank and 18in wheels. Higher gearing to suit the greater torque and power of the 174cc engine, though still three-speed.

Wheelbase	51.1in
Seat height	31in
Ground clearance	5.5in
Overall width	27.75in

Weight (with 1 gallon fuel)

	232lb
Exhaust system	Low level
Colours	

D7 Super, De Luxe & Silver

Bore x stroke	61.5 x 58mm
Capacity	174cc
Compression ratio	7.4:1
Power	7.4bhp @ 4750rpm
Electrical system	Wico-Pacy flywheel magneto, direct lighting
Generator output	30 watts
Battery capacity	11 amp/hour
Ignition timing	0.15625in BTDC
Points gap	0.015in
Sparkplug	Champion L7
Carburettor type	Amal Monobloc 375/31
Choke size	0.875in
Carburettor settings	
Main jet	140
Pilot jet	25
Slide no.	3.5
Needle position	2
Petroil ratio	25:1
Gearbox ratios	
1st	-
2nd	-
3rd	-
Wheel & tyre sizes	
Front	3.00-18 & WM1-18
Rear	3.00-18 & WM1-18
Suspension	
Front	Telescopic forks, hydraulic damping
Rear	Swingarm, twin shocks
Brakes	
Front	Drum, 5.5 x 1in
Rear	Drum, 5.5 x 1in
Sprocket teeth	
Engine	17T
Clutch	38T
Gearbox	16T
Rear wheel	46T
Chains	
Primary size	0.375 x 0.25in,
Primary length	50 links

Super Black or (from 1960), Sapphire Blue or Fuschia Red, all with ivory tank panels with 'Bantam Super' transfers. Royal Red replaces Fuschia Red from 1961. Optional chrome tank panels from 1963.

De Luxe Flamboyant Red or Blue with white lining on mudguards and side panels, chrome tank panels, round silver star acrylic tank badges.

Silver Sapphire Blue, with Polychromatic Silver mudguards, tank panels and headlight

Saddle or dual seat	Dual seat
Notes	Mechanically similar to D5

Super, but with cleaner styling including headlight nacelle incorporating round speedometer. Hydraulically damped forks based on those of the C15, plus bigger 1-inch wide brakes. First use of bright colour options from 1960. De Luxe makes full use of chrome, first Bantam to use kidney-shaped fuel tank and metallic paint, also ball-ended levers and pillion grabstrap on seat. Silver was the cut-price Bantam with less chrome – replaced Super for 1965.

D10 Silver & Supreme 1967 only

Bore x stroke	61.5 x 58mm
Capacity	174cc
Compression ratio	8.65:1
Power	10bhp @ 6000rpm
Electrical system	Wipac alternator, coil ignition, battery lighting
Generator output	60 watts
Battery capacity	11 amp/hour
Ignition timing	0.0625in
Points gap	0.012in
Sparkplug	Champion N4
Carburettor type	Amal Monobloc
Choke size	–
Petroil ratio	25:1
Gearbox ratios	

1st	17.4:1	**Electrical system**	Wipac alternator, coil ignition, battery lighting
2nd	9.3:1		
3rd	6.6:1	**Generator output**	60 watts
Wheel & tyre sizes		**Battery capacity**	11 amp/hour
Front	3.00-18 & WM1-18	**Ignition timing**	0.0625in BTDC
Rear	3.00-18 & WM1-18	**Points gap**	0.012in
Suspension		**Sparkplug**	Champion N4
Front	Telescopic forks, hydraulically damped	**Carburettor type**	Amal Concentric R626/2
		Choke size	26mm
Rear	Swingarm, twin shocks	**Carburettor settings**	
Brakes		Main jet	150
Front	5.5 x 1in	Pilot jet	25
Rear	5.5 x 1in	Slide no.	3
Sprocket teeth		Needle position	2
Engine	17T	**Petroil ratio**	25:1
Gearbox	16T	**Gearbox ratios**	
Clutch chainwheel	38	1st	18.68:1
Rear chainwheel	46T	2nd	12.03:1
Chains		3rd	8.55:1
Primary size	0.375 x 0.25in,	4th	6.57:1
Primary length	50 links	**Wheel & tyre sizes**	
Rear size	0.5 x 0.335in	Front	3.00-18 & WM1-18
Rear length	121 links	Rear	3.00-18 & WM1-18
Capacities		**Suspension**	
Fuel	2 gallons	Front	Telescopic forks, hydraulically damped
Gearbox	0.75 pint		
Dimensions		Rear	Swingarm, twin shocks
Wheelbase	50in	**Brakes**	
Seat height	31in	Front	Drum, 5.5 x 1in
Ground clearance	6,75in	Rear	Drum, 5.5 x 1in
Overall width	27.75in	**Sprocket teeth**	
Weight (with 1 gallon fuel)		Engine	17T
	226lb	Gearbox	16T
Exhaust system	Low level	Clutch chainwheel	38
Colours		Rear chainwheel	46T
Silver	Sapphire Blue, with	**Chains**	

Polychromatic Silver mudguards, tank panels and headlight

Supreme	Flamboyant Blue, chrome	Primary size	0.375 x 0.25in,

tank panels

Saddle or dual seat	Dual seat	Primary length	50 links
Notes	Major upgrade, though	Rear size	0.5 x 0.335in

the D10 itself only lasted a year. Wipac 60-watt alternator, coil ignition and battery lights standard across the range. Higher compression engine with 10bhp. Circular points cover. Silver and Supreme replace previous D7 Silver and De Luxe, and look very similar. A recognition point is the pancake air filter with perforated chrome cover. Silver and De Luxe also retain the three-speed gearbox.

		Rear length	121 links
		Capacities	
		Fuel	1.9 gallons
		Gearbox	0.75 pint
		Dimensions	
		Wheelbase	50in
		Seat height	30.25in
D10 Sports 1967 only		Ground clearance	6.75in
Bore x stroke	61.5 x 58mm	Overall width	23in
Capacity	171cc	**Weight (with 1 gallon fuel)**	
Compression ratio	8.65:1		226lb
Power	10bhp @ 5000rpm	**Exhaust system**	High level

Colours Flamboyant Red, chrome tank panels, black and white chequered trim on tank top, 'Sports' transfers

Saddle or dual seat Humped dual seat

Notes Mechanically similar to

D10 Supreme but with new four-speed gearbox and Amal Concentric carburettor. Cosmetic additions included high-level exhaust, flyscreen, humped seat, full-width hubs, folding kickstart, exposed springs on the rear shocks, flat bars and a rectangular rear numberplate. All set off by chrome on the tank, exhaust heat shields, mudguards, separate headlight and lower forks, plus that black and white trim on the tank.

D10 Bushman 1967 only

Bore x stroke	61.5 x 58mm
Capacity	174cc
Compression ratio	8.65:1
Power	10bhp @ 6000rpm
Electrical system	Wipac alternator, energy transfer ignition
Generator output	60 watts
Battery capacity	N/A
Ignition timing	0.0625in BTDC
Points gap	0.012in
Sparkplug	Champion N4
Carburettor type	Amal Concentric 626/17
Choke size	26mm
Carburettor settings	
Main jet	160
Pilot jet	25
Slide no.	3
Needle position	2
Petroil ratio	25:1
Gearbox ratios	
1st	23.0:1
2nd	14.8:1
3rd	10.5:1
4th	8.1:1
Wheel & tyre sizes	
Front	3.00-19 & WM2-19
Rear	3.00-19 & WM2-19
Suspension	
Front	Telescopic forks, hydraulically damped
Rear	Swingarm, twin shocks
Brakes	
Front	Drum, 5.5 x 1in
Rear	Drum, 5.5 x 1in
Sprocket teeth	
Engine	17T
Gearbox	16T
Clutch chainwheel	38T
Rear chainwheel	58T
Chains	
Primary size	0.375 x 0.25in,
Primary length	50 links
Rear size	0.5 x 0.335in
Rear length	128 links
Capacities	
Fuel	1.9 gallons
Gearbox	0.75 pint
Dimensions	
Wheelbase	50in
Seat height	30.5in
Ground clearance	10.5in
Overall width	27.75in
Weight (with 1 gallon fuel)	
	226lb
Exhaust system	High level
Colours	Bushfire Orange and white tank and centre panels, white mudguards
Saddle or dual seat	Dual seat
Notes	Relatively successful trail bike version of the D10. Not just a cosmetic trailie, but with significantly lower gearing, stronger rear spokes and suspension, high-level exhaust, Dunlop trials tyres and higher, wider bars. Lucas energy transfer ignition avoids the use of a battery. Same four-speed gearbox (though different ratios) as the Sports and Amal Concentric carb (rejetted to suit).

D14/4 1968 to 1969

Bore x stroke	61.5 x 58mm
Capacity	174cc
Compression ratio	10.0:1
Power	12.6bhp @ 5750rpm
Electrical system	Wipac alternator, coil ignition, battery lighting
Generator output	60 watts
Battery capacity	11 amp/hour
Ignition timing	0.0625in BTDC
Points gap	0.012in
Sparkplug	Champion N4
Carburettor type	Amal Concentric R626/2
Choke size	26mm
Carburettor settings	
Main jet	150
Pilot jet	25
Slide no.	3
Needle position	2
Petroil ratio	25:1
Gearbox ratios	
1st	18.68:1
2nd	12.04:1
3rd	8.55:1
4th	6.58:1
Wheel & tyre sizes	
Front	3.00-18 & WM1-18
Rear	3.00-18 & WM1-18
Suspension	
Front	Telescopic forks, hydraulically damped
Rear	Swingarm, twin shocks
Brakes	
Front	Drum, 5.5 x 1in

Rear	Drum, 5.5 x 1in
Sprocket teeth	
Engine	17T
Gearbox	16T
Clutch chainwheel	38T
Rear chainwheel	47T
Chains	
Primary size	0.375 x 0.25in,
Primary length	50 links
Rear size	0.5 x 0.335in
Rear length	120 links
Capacities	
Fuel	1.9 gallons
Gearbox	0.75 pint
Dimensions	
Wheelbase	50in
Seat height	31in
Ground clearance	6.75in
Overall width	27.75in
Weight (with 1 gallon fuel)	
	225lb
Exhaust system	Low level
Colours	Black or Polychromatic Blue

with white lining on mudguards and side panels. 'Yin and yang' paint/chrome on tank

Saddle or dual seat	Dual seat
Notes	Twenty-five per cent more

power from high-compression engine with bigger ports and exhaust pipe. Four-speed gearbox now standard across the range. Bantam Silver dropped, and 14/4 Supreme became entry-level machine. Looked similar to D10 Supreme apart from 'yin-yang' style of paint/chrome on fuel tank. Battery access hole, and clutch adjustment access improved. Air filter now hidden inside right-hand rear panel. Supreme has twin stainless steel mirrors

D14/4 Sports 1968 to 1969

Bore x stroke	61.5 x 58mm
Capacity	174cc
Compression ratio	10.0:1
Power	12.6bhp @ 5750rpm
Electrical system	Wipac alternator, coil ignition, battery lighting
Generator output	60 watts
Battery capacity	11 amp/hour
Ignition timing	0.0625in BTDC
Points gap	0.012in
Sparkplug	Champion N4
Carburettor type	Amal Concentric R626/2
Choke size	26mm
Carburettor settings	
Main jet	150
Pilot jet	25
Slide no.	3
Needle position	2

Petroil ratio	25:1
Gearbox ratios	
1st	18.68:1
2nd	12.04:1
3rd	8.55:1
4th	6.58:1
Wheel & tyre sizes	
Front	3.00-18 & WM1-18
Rear	3.00-18 & WM1-18
Suspension	
Front	Telescopic forks, hydraulically damped
Rear	Swingarm, twin shocks
Brakes	
Front	Drum, 5.5 x 1in
Rear	Drum, 5.5 x 1in
Sprocket teeth	
Engine	17T
Gearbox	16T
Clutch chainwheel	38T
Rear chainwheel	47T
Chains	
Primary size	0.375 x 0.25in,
Primary length	50 links
Rear size	0.5 x 0.335in
Rear length	120 links
Capacities	
Fuel	1.9 gallons
Gearbox	0.75 pint
Dimensions	
Wheelbase	50in
Seat height	31in
Ground clearance	6.75in
Overall width	27.75in
Weight (with 1 gallon fuel)	
	225lb
Exhaust system	Low level
Colours	Flamboyant Red, 'Yin and yang' paint/chrome on tank
Saddle or dual seat	Humped dual seat

D14/4 Bushman 1968 to 1969

Bore x stroke	61.5 x 58mm
Capacity	174cc
Compression ratio	10.0:1
Power	12.6bhp @ 5750rpm
Electrical system	Wipac alternator, coil ignition, battery lighting
Generator output	60 watts
Battery capacity	11 amp/hour
Ignition timing	0.0625in BTDC
Points gap	0.012in
Sparkplug	Champion N4
Carburettor type	Amal Concentric R626/17
Choke size	26mm
Carburettor settings	

Main jet	160
Pilot jet	25
Slide no.	3
Needle position	2
Petroil ratio	25:1
Gearbox ratios	
1st	23.0:1
2nd	14.8:1
3rd	10.5:1
4th	8.1:1
Wheel & tyre sizes	
Front	3.00-19 & WM2-19
Rear	3.00-19 & WM2-19
Suspension	
Front	Telescopic forks, hydraulically damped
Rear	Swingarm, twin shocks
Brakes	
Front	Drum, 5.5 x 1in
Rear	Drum, 5.5 x 1in
Sprocket teeth	
Engine	17T
Gearbox	16T
Clutch chainwheel	38T
Rear chainwheel	58T
Chains	
Primary size	0.375 x 0.25in,
Primary length	50 links
Rear size	0.5 x 0.335in,
Rear length	120 links
Capacities	
Fuel	1.9 gallons
Gearbox	0.75 pint
Dimensions	
Wheelbase	50in
Seat height	31in
Ground clearance	10.5in
Overall width	27.75in
Weight (with 1 gallon fuel)	
	225lb
Exhaust system	High level
Colours	Bushfire Orange and white tank and centre panels, white mudguards
Saddle or dual seat	Dual seat

B175 1969 to 1971

Bore x stroke	61.5 x 58mm
Capacity	174cc
Compression ratio	9.5:1
Power	12.6bhp @ 5750rpm
Electrical system	Wipac alternator, coil ignition, battery lighting
Generator output	60 watts
Battery capacity	11 amp/hour
Ignition timing	0.0625in BTDC
Points gap	0.012in

Sparkplug	Champion N4
Carburettor type	Amal Concentric R626/2
Choke size	26mm
Carburettor settings	
Main jet	150
Pilot jet	25
Slide no.	3
Needle position	2
Petroil ratio	25:1
Gearbox ratios	
1st	18.68:1
2nd	12.04:1
3rd	8.55:1
4th	6.58:1
Wheel & tyre sizes	
Front	3.00-18 & WM1-18
Rear	3.00-18 & WM1-18
Suspension	
Front	Telescopic forks, hydraulically damped
Rear	Swingarm, twin shocks
Brakes	
Front	Drum, 5.5 x 1in
Rear	Drum, 5.5 x 1in
Sprocket teeth	
Engine	17T
Gearbox	16T
Clutch chainwheel	38T
Rear chainwheel	47T
Chains	
Primary size	0.375 x 0.25in,
Primary length	50 links
Rear size	0.5 x 0.335in
Rear length	120 links
Capacities	
Fuel	1.9 gallons
Gearbox	0.75 pint
Dimensions	
Wheelbase	50in
Seat height	31in
Ground clearance	6.75in
Overall width	27.75in
Weight (with 1 gallon fuel)	
	225lb
Exhaust system	Low level
Colours	Flamboyant Blue, with Red or Black options 1970 and Black only for 1971
Saddle or dual seat	Dual seat
Notes	Final Bantam, recognised by new cylinder head with central sparkplug, also stronger bottom end and slightly lower compression. Heavier duty forks from Triumph Sports Cub, with rubber gaiters. Unified threads.

B175 Bushman 1969 to 1971

Bore x stroke	61.5 x 58mm

Capacity	174cc
Compression ratio	9.5:1
Power	12.6bhp @ 5750rpm
Electrical system	Wipac alternator, coil ignition, battery lighting
Generator output	60 watts
Battery capacity	11 amp/hour
Ignition timing	0.0625in
Points gap	0.012in
Sparkplug	Champion N4
Carburettor type	Amal Concentric R626/17
Choke size	26mm
Carburettor settings	
Main jet	160
Pilot jet	25
Slide no.	3
Needle position	2
Petroil ratio	25:1
Gearbox ratios	
1st	23.0:1
2nd	14.8:1
3rd	10.5:1
4th	8.1:1
Wheel & tyre sizes	
Front	3.00-19 & WM2-19
Rear	3.00-19 & WM2-19
Suspension	
Front	Telescopic forks, hydraulically damped
Rear	Swingarm, twin shocks

Brakes	
Front	Drum, 5.5 x 1in
Rear	Drum, 5.5 x 1in
Sprocket teeth	
Engine	17T
Gearbox	16T
Clutch chainwheel	38T
Rear chainwheel	58T
Chains	
Primary size	0.375 x 0.25in,
Primary length	50 links
Rear size	0.5 x 0.335in
Rear length	120 links
Capacities	
Fuel	1.9 gallons
Gearbox	0.75 pint
Dimensions	
Wheelbase	50in
Seat height	31in
Ground clearance	10.5in
Overall width	27.75in
Weight (with 1 gallon fuel)	225lb
Exhaust system	Low level
Colours	Bushfire Orange and white tank and centre panels, white mudguards
Saddle or dual seat	Dual seat
Notes	Short-lived final version of the Bushman, sharing the same engine improvements as the roadster B175, but keeping the Bushman's own features, including Dunlop Trials tyres and bashplate.

Why not visit Veloce on the web? – www.velocebooks.com
New book news • Special offers • Details of all books in print • Gift vouchers

146

Appendix 2: road test data

Bantam D1
The Motor Cycle – 28th October 1948
Speeds in gears
1st 21mph
2nd 41mph
3rd 47mph

Acceleration

	10-20mph	15-25mph	20-30mph
1st	2.8secs	–	–
2nd	3.8secs	4.0secs	3.8secs
3rd	12.6secs	6.2secs	7.6secs

0-30mph through gears 6.6secs
Speed at end of standing ¼-mile: 45mph

Fuel consumption (steady speed)
20mph 192mpg
30mph 160mpg
40mph 128mpg

Braking 30mph to stop	27ft 6in (dry surface)
Turning circle	10ft 5in
Minimum non-snatch speed	12mph in top gear
Weight per cc	1.34lb

Bantam D1 De-Luxe
Motorcycling – 9th February 1950
Speeds in gears
1st –
2nd 37mph
3rd 49mph

Acceleration
Speed at end of standing ¼-mile: 33mph

0-2nd gear maximum 18.2secs
0-3rd gear maximum 48.0secs

Fuel consumption (steady speed)
30mph 179mpg
40mph 115mpg

Braking 30mph to stop	22ft 6in (dry surface)

Bantam D3
The Motor Cycle – 4th March 1954
Speeds in gears
1st 27mph
2nd 38mph
3rd 51mph
Highest one-way speed: 53mph

Acceleration

	10-20mph	15-25mph	20-30mph
1st	2.5secs	3.5secs	–
2nd	3.5secs	3.5secs	3.4secs
3rd	–	6.4secs	6.0secs

0-30mph through gears 6.8secs
Speed at end of standing ¼-mile: 48mph

Fuel consumption (steady speed)
20mph 150mpg
30mph 128mpg
40mph 104mpg

Braking 30mph to stop	36ft (wet surface)
Turning circle	11ft
Minimum non-snatch speed	14mph in top gear
Weight per cc	1.46lb

Bantam D3
Motorcycling – 5th May 1955
Speeds in gears
1st –
2nd 40mph
3rd 51mph

Acceleration
Speed at end of standing ¼-mile: 36mph
Speed at end of flying ¼-mile: 49.4mph

Fuel consumption (steady speed)
At 30mph 165mpg
At 40mph 110mpg

Braking 30mph to stop   29ft (dry surface)

Bantam D3
The Motor Cycle – 5th July 1956
Speeds in gears
1st 22mph
2nd 38mph
3rd 50mph
Highest one-way speed: 52mph

Acceleration

	10-20mph	15-25mph	20-30mph
1st	3.0secs	–	–
2nd	3.6secs	3.6secs	4.0secs
3rd	–	6.4secs	6.6secs

0-30mph through gears 7.1secs
Speed at end of standing ¼-mile: 49mph

Fuel consumption (steady speed)
At 20mph 165mpg
At 30mph 145mpg
At 40mph 95mpg

Braking 30mph to stop   36ft (dry surface)
Turning circle   13ft 10in
Minimum non-snatch speed   15mph in top gear
Weight per cc   1.54lb

Bantam D5 Super
The Motor Cycle – 13th March 1958
Speeds in gears
1st 26mph
2nd 43mph
3rd 57mph
Highest one-way speed: 59mph

Acceleration

	10-20mph	15-25mph	20-30mph
1st	2.4secs	–	–
2nd	3.6secs	3.8secs	5.8secs
3rd	–	6.0secs	8.0secs

Speed at end of standing ¼-mile: 49mph
Time at end of standing ¼-mile: 24 secs

Fuel consumption (steady speed)
At 30mph 150mpg
At 40mph 112mpg
At 50mph 92mpg

Braking 30mph to stop   34ft (dry surface)
Turning circle   12ft 8in
Minimum non-snatch speed   15mph in top gear
Weight per cc   1.35lb

Bantam D7 Super
The Motor Cycle – 12th March 1964
Speeds in gears
1st 23mph
2nd 42mph
3rd 54mph
Highest one-way speed: 56mph

Acceleration

	10-20mph	15-25mph	20-30mph
1st	2.6secs	–	–
2nd	3.2secs	4.0secs	6.0secs
3rd	–	6.4secs	6.8secs

0-30mph through gears 7.1secs
Speed at end of standing ¼-mile: 49mph

Fuel consumption (steady speed)
At 30mph 136mpg
At 40mph 125mpg
At 50mph 82mpg

Braking 30mph to stop   33ft (dry surface)
Turning circle   12ft 8in
Minimum non-snatch speed   18mph in top gear
Weight per cc   1.34lb

Bantam D10 Sports
Motorcycle Mechanics – April 1967
Speeds in gears
1st 20mph
2nd 40mph
3rd 50mph
4th 62mph

Acceleration
0-10mph 2.0secs
0-30mph 5.9secs
0-50mph 15.9secs
Standing ¼-mile: 25.3secs (terminal speed, 57.6mph)

Fuel consumption
In town – 92mpg

Touring – 113mpg
Overall – 90mpg

Braking 30mph to stop   33ft (damp surface)
Turning circle   11ft 9in
Minimum non-snatch speed 15mph in top gear

Bantam D14/4 Supreme
Motorcycle Mechanics – October 1968
Speeds in gears
1st 17mph
2nd 42mph
3rd 54mph
4th 62mph

Acceleration
0-30mph 4.1secs
0-40mph 6.5secs
0-50mph 10.2secs
0-60mph 14.4secs

Fuel consumption
Hard riding – 70mpg
Touring – 92mpg
Overall – 78mpg

Braking 30mph to stop   29ft 6in (dry surface)

Minimum non-snatch speed 17mph in top gear

Bantam B175
The Motor Cycle – 26th February 1969
Speeds in gears
1st 22mph
2nd 34mph
3rd 42mph*
4th 65mph
Highest one-way speed: 66mph

Acceleration
0-30mph 4.7secs
0-40mph 7.2secs
0-50mph 11.5secs
Standing ¼-mile: 23.0secs
(terminal speed: 58.0mph)

Fuel consumption
Overall – 86mpg

Braking 30mph to stop 30ft (dry surface)
Turning circle 12ft 6in
Minimum non-snatch speed 22mph in top gear
Weight per cc 1.8lb

Probably an error

Why not visit Veloce on the web? – www.velocebooks.com
New book news • Special offers • Details of all books in print • Gift vouchers

149

Appendix 3: year-by-year changes

Years refer to model years, which usually began in October, but could start as early as August.

Year Changes

1948 Bantam D1 introduced. Fork gaiters added after intitial production batches.

1949 D1 Competition introduced. Plunger frame option introduced ('S' suffix in frame number). Bantam cockrell transfer on tank. Centre stand secured by C-shaped link and spring instead of clip. Modification to front hub – deep counter bore to aid bearing removal is deleted from frame YD-2851.

1950 D1 De Luxe introduced, with Lucas 1A45 generator/battery lighting and plunger frame as standard. Exhaust pipe moved from under to over footrest from frame YD24813. Plunger frame optional on standard D1.

1951 Wico-Pacy series 55 Mk8 generator replaces Geni-mag type from engine YD1-40661. Fork bushes detachable from frame YD1-57331 (rigid) and YD1S-57331 (plunger). Revised cable-operated lighting switch on handlebar. D1 De Luxe now has electric horn, with button on handlebar. On all bikes, Amal 361/1 carburettor replaces 261/001D, and pull and turn fuel tap replaces push-pull type.

1952 Steering headstock has strengthened gusset. Headlight switch fitted to direct lighting (ie non-De Luxe) models).

1953 D1 De Luxe discontinued. Big-end redesigned with crowded rollers. Now 13 crankcase screws (was 11). Engine number now stamped on crankcase under carburettor. Pillion footrests now standard and dual seat optional. Wheel rims chromed and chrome strips on tank seams. Bigger rear wheel spindle on plunger frame. New front mudguard with slimmer valancing, bolted to lower fork stanchions.

1954 Bantam Major introduced. All engines now with large fins and thick-rim flywheels (similar to that used on Lucas-equipped De Luxe). Left-hand crank seal moved 0.01in outwards and right-hand seal now positioned against flywheel. New oilway drillings allow gearbox oil to lubricate right-hand main bearing. Tubular silencer replaces fishtail type. Three-bulb stop/tail light on battery-equipped bikes. Positive earth electrics. Rubber damping on all forks. Fuel filler cap moved to right-hand side. D3: Heavier forks. D1: New headlight cowl.

1955 Cylinder barrel and head stud centres increased to 55mm. Circlip fitted to left-hand crankcase seal.

1956 D1 Competition & rigid frame discontinued. D1 engines have shims fitted to left-hand main bearing. D3 swingarm frame introduced and D3 plunger discontinued. Crankshaft oil drag fan replaces plain collar.

1957 On all engines, left-hand main bearing seal fitted against flywheel, and extra left-hand seal added. Oilway drillings allow gearbox oil to reach left-hand main bearing.

1958 D5 Super introduced, D3 Major discontinued. New big-end bearing with Duralamin cages and radial drillings in con-rod for all engines. D5: Crankcase studs moved out to 60mm.

1959 D7 Super introduced, D5 Super discontinued. New frame and side panels, cleaner look, newseat, headlight nacelle with circular speedometer, hydraulically-damped forks, bigger brakes, brighter colours. 'Super' script on left-hand outer engine cover.

1960 D1: Frame, forks and headlight now painted black. D7: Padlock lugs fitted to frame and lower steering yoke.

1961 Acrylic pear-shaped 'BSA' badges on fuel tank. Gold-lined chrome tank panels optional.

1962 Torrington needle-roller small-end replaces bronze bush on D7. Three extra crankcase screws, one under the top rear-mounting bolt. Gearbox ratios revised and splines on gear shafts changed. Rear sprocket now 47 teeth (was 46). New silencer, retained by two bolts. Front mudguard with two fixing holes and revised rear mudgard. New rear numberplate with rear light at the top. Left-hand side panel, the battery carrier and rear chainguard all changed. Handlebar bend changed, with option of higher rise.

1963 D1 discontinued. Magnetic speedometers introduced, revised silencer.

1964 Revised big-end with improved lubrication. Stub form tooth profiles for gearbox.

1965 D7 De Luxe introduced: New kidney-shaped 1.9-gallon fuel tank with chrome panels, two top seams with chrome strips, central filler cap. Black dual seat with red piping and grabstrap. Ball-ended levers. Battery lighting form only, with external ignition coil and extra ignition switch on headlight (ditto D7 Super battery model). New silencer with black unfinned end cap. De Luxe in Flamboyant Red with white pinstriping on mudguards, and polished side cases.

1966 D7 Super discontinued. D7 Silver introduced, Sapphire Blue finish and polychromatic silver mudguards, headlight cowl and fuel tank side panels. Dual seat with white piping and no grabstrap.

1967 D10 introduced, D7 discontinued. D10 Silver replaces D7 Silver. D10 Supreme replaces D7 De Luxe. New D10 Sports with Amal Concentric carb, high-level exhaust, flat bars, four-speed gearbox, full-width hubs, exposed springs, humped seat, flyscreen, metallic paint, chequered tank trim and lots of chrome. D10 Bushman dual-purpose on/off road with Amal Concentric carb, four-speed gearbox, high-level exhaust, lower gearing, knobbly tyres (larger section rear), wide bars, Bushfire Orange and white finish. All D10s have high-compression engine with 10bhp and 60-watt Wipac alternator electrics. All coil ignition except Bushman (energy discharge type).

1968 D14/4 introduced, D10 range discontinued. D14/4 Supreme, Sports and Bushman replace D10 equivalents, all with 12.6bhp 10:1 compression engine with bigger ports and larger exhaust pipe. Air filter hidden inside right-hand side panel. Four-speed gearbox and Amal Concentric carb fitted to all models. Access hole for battery. Supreme: 'yin/yang' paint/chrome on fuel tank, seat with marble top finish, white piping and chrome strip around base. D14/4 Sports: one-piece exhaust heat shield, new front mudguard, heavier front fork with thicker stanchions, welded-on mudguard stay and clipless rubber gaiters. Front brake backplate has anchor arm located to lug cast in fork leg. D14/4 Bushman: same fork as Sports.

1969 B175 introduced, D14/4 range discontinued. Stronger bottom end (more secure compression discs, stiffer crankshaft, bigger gudgeon pin and small-end, 17 crankcase fixing screws), new cylinder-head with central sparkplug, slightly lower compression. New front fork from Triumph Sports Cub, with gaiters, new mudguards, silencer mounting, left-hand side panel and exposed rear shock springs. UNF threads.

1970 No changes.

March 1971   B175 discontinued.

Appendix 4: Bantam contacts

Clubs all over the world, spares specialists, useful websites, addresses and books.

CLUBS

Bantam Racing
www.bsabantamracing.co.uk

BSA Bantam Club
Mike Kilvert 01686 610093 mike.kilvert@btinternet.com

BSA Bantam Virtual Club
www.communigate.co.uk/ne/bsabantamvc

BSA Owners Club (UK)
www.bsaoc.demon.co.uk
www.bsaoc.org

British Two-Stroke Club (UK)
www.btsc.btinternet.co.uk

Australia – New South Wales
www.bsansw.org.au

Australia – South Australia
www.geocities.com/neds1au/default.htm

Belgium
www.bsaoc.be

Canada
www.geocities.com/MotorCity/Pit/8053

Czech Republic
www.bsa.webpark.cz

Denmark
www.bsa.dk

France
Thierry Berthelot, Varaaize 17400, Saint Jean D'Angely, France

Germany
www.bsa-oc.de

Italy
Mario Di Giovanni, Via Cologno Mon Sese 174, 00135 Roma, Italy

Luxembourg
Gilbert Bredims, 23 Dreikantonstross, L 8352, Dahlem, Luxembourg

Netherlands
www.bsa-oc.com

New Zealand
Robert Cochrane, PO Box 33-018, Petone, Wellington, New Zealand

Norway
www.bsaoc.no

Portugal
Paulo Mendes, Apartado 6060, P-9001-501 Funchal, Portugal

Switzerland
Email: hrvr@kfn-ag.ch

USA
www.bsaoc.org

SPECIALISTS

There are so many BSA specialists out there that it would be impossible to list them all, so listing is restricted to UK companies. Many others (including some here) are not specialists but still stock a good line of Bantam spares. This list does not imply recommendation and is not deemed to be comprehensive. Most of the companies listed offer a worldwide mail order service.

A Gagg & Sons
Spares – Nottingham
www.gagg-and-sons.freeserve.co.uk 0115 9786288

Autocycle Engineering
Spares – West Midlands
01384 253030

Britbits
Spares – Bournemouth
www.britbits.co.uk 01202 483675

Burlen Fuel Sytems
Amal carburettor spares
www.burlen.co.uk 01722 412500

C&D Autos
Spares – Birmingham
0121 706 2902 Email
canddautos@eidosnet.co.uk

Draganfly Motorcycles
Spares – Norfolk
www.draganfly.co.uk 01986
894798

Kidderminster Motorcycles
Spares – Herefordshire
01562 66679

Len Baker
Spares – Suffolk
01502 724488

Lightning Spares
Spares – Cheshire
0161 969 3850

Malcolm Leech
Electrical parts – Birmingham
0121 559 7306

Sheffield British Motorcycles
'Bantam John' – Sheffield
01246 290021

SRM Engineering
Spares/engineering/restorations
– Aberystwyth
www.srm-engineering.com
01970 627771

Supreme Motorcycles
Spares – Leicestershire
www.suprememotorcycles.co.uk
01455 841133

T&G Motorcycles
Spares – Buckinghamshire
01908 579799

BIBLIOGRAPHY
Books
British Motorcycles Since 1950, Vols 1 & 2, Steve Wilson, Patrick Stephens Limited, 1991
BSA Bantam: All Models, Roy Bacon, Nitor Publishing, 1990
BSA Bantam – The Essential Buyers Guide, Peter Henshaw, Veloce Publishing, 2008
BSA Bantam Super Profile, Jeff Clew, Haynes, 1983
BSA Competition History, Norman Vanhouse, Haynes, 1986
BSA Instruction Manual (small format, c50 pages, found at autojumbles)
BSA Twins and Triples, Roy Bacon, Haynes
Riding the Wall of Death, Ford, Allan & Nick Corble, Tempus, 2006
The Illustrated History of BSA Motorcycles, Roy Bacon, Promotional Reprint Company, 1995
Great British Bikes of the Sixties, Bob Currie, Chancellor Press, 2000
The Book of the BSA Bantam, Pitman's Motor-Cyclists' Library (again, found at autojumbles)
Haynes Owners Workshop Manual: BSA Bantam, Manual No0117, Haynes Publishing
Practical British Lightweight Two-Stroke Motorcycles, Steve Wilson, Haynes Publishing, 1990
BSA Bantam, Owen Wright, Crowood Press, 2003
The Giants of Small Heath, Barry Ryerson, GT Foulis
The Triumph Tiger Cub Bible, Mike Estall, Veloce Publishing, 2000
TT Topics & Tales, David Wright

Magazines
British Bike Magazine
Classic Bike
Classic Motorcycle Mechanics
Motorcycle Sport & Leisure
Motorcycling
The Classic Motorcycle
The Motor Cycle

Appendix 5: engine/frame numbers

Engine/frame numbers from factory despatch records *(not complete, some gaps)* –

ENGINE

Date	Engine number	Model
9.47-2.48	D18351-18678	D1 GPO
12.48-5.50	101-6393	
9.49-8.50	D20001-38657	
1.50-8.50	YDL101-2950	
11.49-3.51	D122001-122675	D1 GPO
9.50-8.51	D40001-60968	
9.51	D8055-8452	
9.51-6.52	D6097-75469	
2-9.52	D122811-123590	D1 GPO
5-10.52	D75470-81412	
3-11.52	D10976-13652	
7.53-6.57	D5001-7150	D1 GPO
8.54-12.55	DDB101-4137 *(some gaps)*	D1
11.57-3.58	D8301-10370	D1 GPO
3.59-9.65	D11401-D19195	D1 GPO
1.67	D101-300	HD7
11.57-7.68	D101-365	No prefix

FRAME

Date	Engine number	Model
11.57-11.58	D101-8521	D5
12.58-3.60	??-D14203	D7
3.60-2.61	D14204-22417	D7
1.61-3.62	D22418-30645	D7
3.62-1.65	D30646-45119	D7
1.65-11.65	D45120-52037	D7
11.65-6.66	GD101-8392	D7
6.66-7.66	GD8393-8618	D7
7.66	9268	
7.66-9.67	D103-8436	D10
7.67-12.67	D8437-8947	D10
11.67-6.68	D101-8352	D13 & 14
6.68-3.69	D8353-13839	D14
17.11.69-		
15.9.71	104-7892	B175

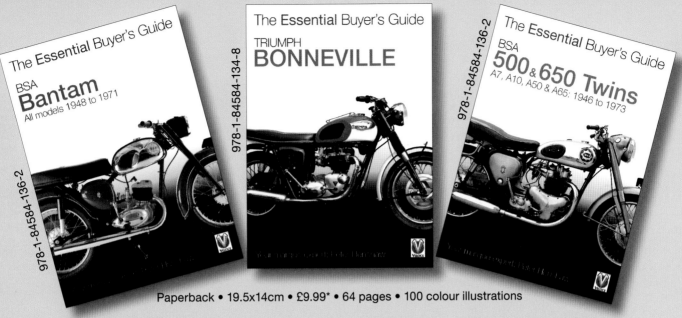
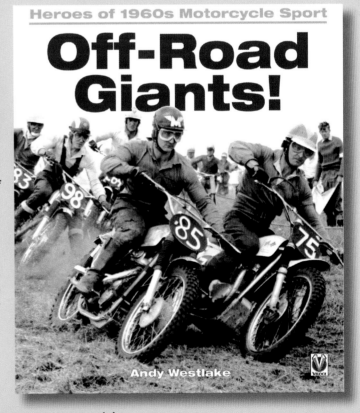

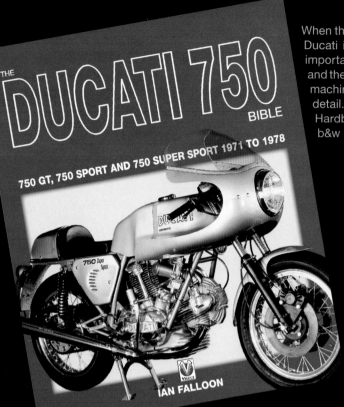

When the great Ducati engineer Fabio Taglioni designed the 750 Ducati in 1970 there was no way he could comprehend how important this model would be. The 750, the Formula 750 racer and the Super Sport became legend: this book celebrates these machines. Year-by-year, model-by-model, change-by-change detail.

Hardback • 25x20.7cm • £29.99* • 160 pages • 163 colour & b&w illustrations. ISBN: 978-1-845840-12-9

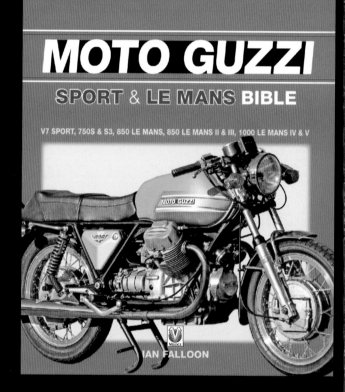

The Moto Guzzi V7 Sport and Le Mans are iconic sporting motorcycles of the 1970s and 1980s. Covering the period 1971-1993, and all models with a description of model development year-by-year, full production data and 160 photos, this is a highly informative book and an essential Bible for enthusiasts.

Hardback • 25x20.7cm • £29.99* • 160 pages • 160 colour & b&w illustrations. ISBN: 978-1-845840-64-8

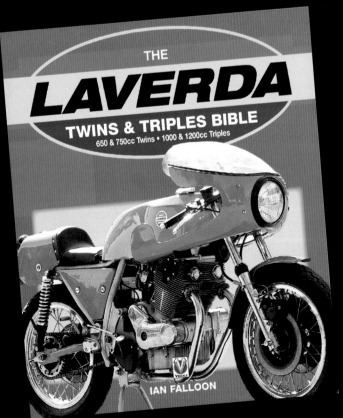

The large capacity Laverda twins and triples were some of the most charismatic and exciting motorcycles produced in a golden era. With a successful endurance racing program publicizing them, Laverda's twins soon earned a reputation for durability. Here is the year-by-year, model-by-model, change-by-change record.

Hardback • 25x20.7cm • £29.99* • 160 pages • 222 colour & b&w illustrations. ISBN: 978-1-845840-58-7

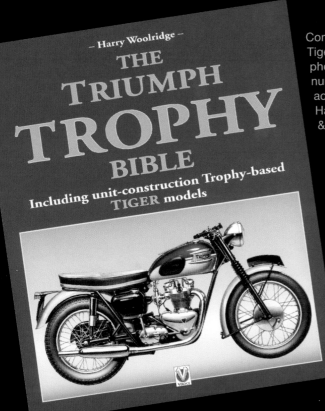

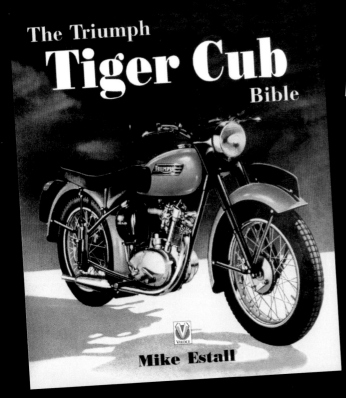

Index